REVIVA
A NEEDED PARADIGM S

Table of Contents

Preface

PREFACE

You may rightly ask, "Do we need another book on prayer?" I say, "Yes. We must. We are doomed without revival and revival comes only through revival prayer and revival prayer comes only when we are willing to pay the price for it. Consider the words which summarize the end for the nation of Judah. "The Lord, the God of their fathers, sent word to them again and again by His messengers, because He had compassion on His people and on His dwelling place; but they continually mocked the messengers of God, despised His words and scoffed at His prophets, until the wrath of the Lord arose against His people, until there was no remedy (2 Chronicles 36:15-16).

Can there be a more sad, sordid description of a once great nation! Israel, the apple of God's eye, the people with whom He had made covenant, those whom He had loved with an everlasting love, were invaded by the wicked Babylonians under King Nebuchadnezzar and taken away into exile. The final invasion came in 586 B.C. but had been going on for nearly twenty years. The northern kingdom of Israel was long gone, having been destroyed under the Assyrians in 722 B.C. The young men of Judah were slain by the sword, and Nebuchadnezzar showed no compassion toward young man or virgin, nor toward old men or the infirm. All the articles of the house of the Lord were taken, and they burned the temple with fire. Those who escaped the sword were carried away to Babylonian exile and became slaves. Why? God had sent them prophets like Isaiah, Amos, Hosea, Jeremiah, Ezekiel, and Daniel, but they mocked His messengers. They despised the words of the prophets. So God's wrath was poured out upon them until there was no remedy, until there was no way of escape.

John Winthrop's coming to Massachusetts Bay in 1630 with his Puritan vision of a "City on a Hill" was driven by strong gospel preaching by men like Thomas Hooker and Increase and Cotton Mather. But by 1675 this was already "going south" with worldliness, ambivalence, and spiritual infidelity. So, in judgment, God sent them Metacomet, chief of the Algonquians, who wrought havoc in Connecticut, wiping out six towns, killing thousands of settlers. In the eighteenth century God sent us more great prophetic preachers—men like George Whitefield, Jonathan Edwards, and William and Gilbert Tennent; and we listened to them for a while, from around 1735 to 1760, but then we grew tired of their preaching, preferring a watered down, Deistic message. So, in judgment, God sent us the Enlightenment of skeptics like David Hume, Jean Jacques Rousseau, and the Marquis de Sade. America has never really recovered from the Enlightenment. In the nineteenth century God, in mercy, sent us many great preachers— men like Asahel Nettleton, James Henley Thornwell, and Daniel Baker; and for a while we listened to them too, giving us the Second Great Awakening from 1800 to 1840 and the 1859 revival as well. But we soon preferred Charles Darwin's teaching (1859, *Origin of Species*) to gospel truth. So God, in judgment, sent us the *War Between the States,* resulting in the death of over 600,000 young men on the battlefields of places like Gettysburg, Bull Run, and Shiloh (by comparison we lost 405,000 in World War II and 53,000 in the Viet Nam War). And in the twentieth century God, in mercy, sent us great prophetic preachers like J. Gresham Machen, Francis Schaeffer, Billy Graham, and Martyn Lloyd-Jones but we refused to listen to them too. So God, in judgment, brought us the bloodiest century in the history of the world with millions dying at Somme, Iwo Jima, Auschwitz, Inchon, Saigon, Mosul, and abortion mills which continue to murder the unborn. And now, here we are in the twenty-first century, and where are the prophets? Where are God's messengers who command a huge, nationwide audience, who can transform a single nation by their preaching? I am not saying we do not have many, many fine, popular and skilled preachers; but where are the prophets of old?

2

My brethren—God has always used revival preaching, and unless He brings it again I fear we are doomed as a civilization. Regardless of whether you like or despise what happens in national, state, or local elections, our hope is not in government. Our help is in the name of the Lord who made heaven and earth (Psalm 121:1). I have often said, "Without revival, we are doomed," but what specifically do I mean by this statement? Well, obviously I am not a prophet nor the son of a prophet, so anything I write here is speculation; but surely we can read the signs of the times and venture on what we now see. Surely without revival leading to wholesale repentance the judgment must come. How can God not judge the United States for our shameless murder of millions of infants, the utter disregard for the sanctity of marriage, and the perversion known as "same sex marriage." If He judged Sodom then surely He must judge us! Often judgment in Scripture takes the form of calamity in natural catastrophes. The plague that killed thousands comes immediately to mind (Numbers 16:41ff). We have had unprecedented natural disasters in the last few years. Perhaps these will continue with even greater intensity and frequency. Then surely the rising threat of nuclear war in the middle east is upon us. Iran with nuclear weapons is an incredibly destabilizing force. And we must never forget Islam's desire to conquer. The Muslims have no intention of peacefully co-existing with anyone of any other religious or political persuasion. They want to conquer America. They love to purchase vacated church buildings and put mosques in them. They are all about symbolism. Perhaps you believe that I am overstating the case to say that Islam can overrun this nation. I am sure Augustine never believed something like Islam could conquer North Africa but it did within four hundred years of his death. Unless revival comes, yielding thousands of conversions among former Muslims, then Islam dominating western Europe is a foregone conclusion. The average western European family has 1.7 children while the Muslims have eight children. Unless the Muslims come to Christ, then western Europe will be Muslim within fifty years. Many in the Netherlands and Germany are speaking out against this but it may be "too little, too late."

Then, unless there is a very quick reversal in the growing debt problem in our nation, an economic meltdown of unprecedented proportions is inevitable. This is mindless and utterly irresponsible. Recently the Federal Reserve quietly instituted round three of Quantitative Easing (QE3), a move to print more money to stimulate the sluggish economic recovery. This weakens the dollar and is one of the reasons for the increase in gasoline prices. The dollar is weak against commodities and other currencies. Without a significant reversal we are bound eventually to have hyper, hyper inflation and utter chaos. And then there is the problem of the "haves and the have nots" in our society. The friction continues to grow and I fear violence in the streets along ethnic, racial, and socio-economic lines.

What, then, must we do? We need an intolerable burden, an intense grief over the status quo in our personal lives, in the church, and in the world. This must drive us to revival prayer, asking God to raise up mighty preachers who can address our entire nation. They are likely to be "nobodies from nowhere," probably young men, probably those totally unexpected. But we need them—men possessed by the Spirit, fearless men who love Jesus more than their lives, men upon whom the Holy Spirit rests with great power and authority. "O God, would you revive your work in the midst of the years. In wrath, O Lord, would you remember mercy," (Habakkuk 3:2).

So this, another book on prayer, is needed because we need a more fervent, more virile type of prayer. We need revival prayer. My intention is to address this issue in four main divisions. First, I will lay down the foundation for revival prayer, stressing two vital ingredients. We must gain and maintain an intolerable burden, and we must have a true, profound, experiential humiliation for our sin, leading us to sincere repentance that alters our thinking, speech, values, and actions. Second, I hope to explain what I mean by revival. After all, there is much confusion on the topic. The term "revival" to some conjures up old time, tent meetings with saw dust on the floor; but that is not what I mean by revival. Revival is a Biblical term and I hope to define it in three ways. First we will look at this exegetically, by explaining and applying Psalm 85. Second, we will illustrate this exegetical idea of revival by looking at some of the great revivals in the history of the church. And third, we will address the issue of revival topically. I will show the ten marks of a revival culture, putting forth the notion that these are normative for every church in every nation.

The third main division of the book asks the question, "What is Revival Prayer?" I will put forth the principle of making your church a house of prayer for the nations. I will briefly note the twin pillars on which the house of prayer for the nations must be built, and then I will lay out the twelve living stones that make up this house of prayer. And fourth and finally, I will give practical guidelines for conducting weekends of Revival Prayer, and show how to keep weekly Revival Prayer going in the church. I will also give some very practical ways to pray for the lost, for our missionaries, for church officers, etc.

I have been conducting Days of Revival Prayer around the United States and world with my friend and mentor Henry Krabbendam, and I often have people ask me for my notes. I believe it is now time to make them available to people, so what follows is what I teach on these days of Revival Prayer. My objective, in writing this book, and in continually conducting Days of Revival Prayer is that we will realize our vital necessity for a major paradigm shift in the church. Business as usual is not working. The preaching, planning, and programs of today's church are not changing our culture. The church of Jesus is increasingly irrelevant in today's western world. This book is my humble effort to see God once again pour out His Holy Spirit, to convict and convert millions, to show forth the powerful, life-changing message of Jesus Christ.

DEDICATION

I joyfully dedicate this book to my long time friend and mentor, Dr. Henry Krabbendam. I first met Henry in 1978 while he was a professor at Covenant College and I was working with youth at First Presbyterian Church, Macon, GA. We had Henry conduct a week long youth evangelistic program with powerful results. Since then we have labored together in preaching, teaching, praying, and evangelizing in many parts of the United States and Africa. Without hesitation or hyperbole, I must say that nearly all I know in ministry concerning zeal, passion, vision, prayer, preaching, and gospel holiness I owe to Henry Krabbendam. I don't know of a man who better combines a keen, theological mind with zeal and holiness, along with powerful preaching and teaching like Henry. Henry you are a great joy to me, and thank you for the countless hours you have spent teaching, modeling, and living out the fullness of the Spirit.

Part I: THE FOUNDATION FOR REVIVAL PRAYER

Chapter 1
The Intolerable Burden

. . . but to this one I will look, to him who is humble and contrite of spirit, and who trembles at my word, Isaiah 66:2.

When the Puritans came to the Massachusetts Bay in 1630 under the leadership of John Winthrop, they came humbly, expectantly, seeking earnestly to fear and honor God, to forge out of this new land a city on a hill. They established Harvard by 1638 for the purpose of training men for the gospel ministry. They had mighty preachers in their early years, men like John Cotton, Thomas Hooker, Increase Mather, and Cotton Mather. They had lived peacefully with the Indian tribes in southern New England for forty years, but they soon began to have problems with Metacomet, the Chief of the Algonquian nation. They referred to Metacomet as King Philip and by 1675 the king of the Algonquians was sending his warriors on killing rampages in Massachusetts and Connecticut. Per capita this brief war was the bloodiest in American history. By the time the English settlers had Metacomet's head on a plate, thousands of men, women, and children were dead. At least six towns in Connecticut were totally wiped out. Some thirty years earlier Thomas Hooker sent one hundred men from Hartford to attack the Pequots who had been killing people from Lyme up to Wethersfield, CT. , but King Phillip's killing spree was far worse. As the settlers fought back many of their ministers were appalled at the violence and bloodthirstiness they saw in the civilized, Puritan settlers. They were no better than the heathen savages. In fact one of the ministers wrote at the time: "We are a people in extreme danger of perishing in our own sins and under God's judgments. All ordinary means of promoting moral reformation have failed, causing us to ask ourselves whether our degeneracy and apostasy may not prove to be perpetual."[1]

This sad reality drove the people to repent, to humble themselves under the mighty hand of God, to tremble at the word of God. This is what Isaiah is after as he calls the nation of Israel to repent and turn from idolatry to faith in the true and living God, Yahweh. He is the great and mighty One, the God of covenantal mercies, who shows lovingkindness to thousands, but who will by no means leave the guilty unpunished (Exodus 34:6-7).

What happened as these Puritans prayed in repentance? By 1735 the Holy Spirit came powerfully upon the preaching of Jonathan Edwards in Northampton, MA. At least fifteen were converted weekly from January to June. Some thought that perhaps all had been converted in the town. At the same time in England and Wales, God saved three men within two months of each other—George Whitefield, Howell Harris, and Daniel Rowland— who all became mighty instruments of revival in their day. Vast hoards of people heard these men and were saved. This brought a mighty societal impact in England, Scotland, Wales, and the American Colonies which averted the ravages of the godless French Revolution of 1789 that gave us Robespierre and the guillotine. Could it be that the humiliation through which the Puritans in 1675 went was the catalyst to drive them to seek God earnestly, which eventually brought the Great Awakening some sixty years later!

---

[1] Cited by Joel Rosenberg in his book *Implosion: Can America Recover from Its Economic and Spiritual Challenges in Time?* Pages 232-233

My brethren, should we not confess how vile, wicked, and perverse we are as a nation? We rightfully grieve the three thousand who died on September 11, 2001 in the Twin Towers in Manhattan, but let us not forget that three thousand die everyday from abortion in the U.S. The owner of the largest abortion mill in Florida has said that young women from evangelical churches in his city are the majority of his clients. Evangelicals talk of the sanctity of heterosexual marriage in condemning same sex marriages, but our divorce rate is as high, if not higher, than secular people in our culture. There are church officers in evangelical churches who are members of the Aryan nation movement. I am told that the vast majority of young men making application to a particular ministry as full time workers are addicted to pornography. The words of Jesus to the church at Sardis are true of the evangelical church today. "We have a name that we are alive but we are dead," (Revelation 3:1). Can we not agree, therefore, that our ordinary means of promoting moral reformation has failed? Business as usual is not working. We have never had more money, more preachers, more education, more planning than today, but we continue to lose ground. Should we not ask ourselves if we too are perpetually in a state of degeneracy and apostasy?

What, then, must we do? We must gain an intolerable burden. Until we have it, nothing else we do will avail much at all. We can go on with our planning, programs, personalities, building, and budgets but we will continue to lose ground in our culture. Without the intolerable burden we are kidding ourselves. This is absolutely essential. Okay, what is the intolerable burden? I define it as an intense grief with the status quo in our personal lives, in the church, and in the world. The Scriptures are replete with men and women who exhibit the intolerable burden. Take Daniel, a contemporary of Jeremiah and Ezekiel, for example. By the ninth chapter of his prophecy he tells us that he is reading the prophet Jeremiah who prophesies a return from the Babylonian captivity in seventy years (Daniel 9:2, Jeremiah 25:11-12, 29:10). This revelation serves at least two purposes in his life. First, it is like a life-line to a drowning man. There he is, in dismay, discouragement, and devastation; having witnessed firsthand the devastation of Judah by Nebuchadnezzar and his hoards. Daniel knows the judgment is just, but he nonetheless, in exile himself, is deeply burdened. So he begins to seek God by prayer and supplications (earnest and fervent prayer), with fasting, sackcloth, and ashes, confessing his own sins and the sins of the people. He says, "We have sinned, committed iniquity, turning aside from Your commandments and ordinances." He goes on to say, "Righteousness belongs to You, O Lord, but to us open shame." He goes still further, beseeching the Lord, "Let now Your anger and Your wrath turn away from Your city Jerusalem, Your holy mountain." He asks the Lord to hear his prayer, to shine His face on the people, to incline His ear, to see the desolation of the city. He appeals, not to any merits in himself or the people, for they have none. Rather he appeals to the Lord's great compassion (Daniel 9:4-19). His intense grief over the status quo drives Daniel to contrition, confession, supplication, and intercession.

We see the same thing with Ezra. Judah had been brought back into the land in 536 B.C. by a decree of King Cyrus of the Medo-Persian Empire which had recently overrun the Babylonian Empire. The people of Judah began immediately to rebuild the temple but were discouraged by local opposition and quit. At least one hundred years passed with Judah "living large" in the land of their forefathers, but still having done nothing to rebuild the temple. Finally God raised up a prophet, Haggai, who declares to God's people that it is now time for the house of the Lord to be rebuilt. He charged Israel with paneling their own dens while the Lord's house remained desolate (Haggai 1:2-6). Ezra and the people were brought to the place of an intolerable burden. They could no longer stand the status quo. Something must be done. They must rebuild the temple, which they did with great fervor, sacrifice, and zeal. The people rejoiced at the great things God had done through them (Ezra 6:13-18). Sometime later Ezra heard that many of the people, even after all Yahweh had done for them—making a covenant with their father Abraham, David, and Solomon; after hearing their cries for deliverance from Egyptian bondage, and the hardships of wicked rulers in the time of the Judges; after bringing them back into the promised land; even after mercifully delivering them from the Babylonian captivity; even after enabling them to rebuild the temple—were still giving their children to be married to pagans. In fact the princes and rulers of Israel were foremost in this unfaithfulness to Yahweh's covenant (Ezra 9:1-4). Ezra cannot believe it! When he heard of it he tore his robe and pulled the hair from his head and beard and sat down appalled. When the people saw Ezra's response to their infidelity they trembled at the words of God on account of their unfaithfulness. He is beside himself with grief. Ezra had the intolerable burden. He could not stand the status quo.

Furthermore, we see the same thing in Nehemiah, another contemporary of Ezra. He was living in Medo-Persia, the cupbearer to the king. In other words, he was a man in high position, a trustworthy man. Perhaps he had heard before of the continued desolation in Jerusalem. Perhaps not. At any rate, he asks how things are going and he is told that after all these years of being back in the land from the exile, perhaps as many as one hundred years, the people there are in great distress and reproach, and the wall around the city is still broken down. Anyone living at the time would clearly understand the vital necessity of a city wall for defense. Without it, a city could easily be overrun and sacked by an enemy. Hanani, Nehemiah's brother, gives him the bad news but this does not seem to bother Hanani one bit, or the others who are with him. However, this news greatly grieved Nehemiah. When he heard these words he sat down and wept and mourned for days. He goes on to say that he was fasting and praying before the Lord, beseeching the awesome God who preserves covenant and lovingkindness for those who love Him and keep His commandments. He goes on to confess the sins of his fathers, reminding Yahweh of His promise to gather His people if they return to Him, if they keep His commandments. He asks Yahweh to grant him favor and compassion before King Artaxerxes (Nehemiah 1:5-11). We know the story. The king grants him favor, allowing Nehemiah to return to Jerusalem. Eventually he rebuilds the wall in fifty-two days. He returns to Medo-Persia and serves there again for many years. Finally, Nehemiah returns to Jerusalem as the governor and continues making vital reforms. He tells us in Nehemiah 13 that he expelled Tobiah, a troubler of God's people, from temple duty and privileges. He also restored the tithe. The faithlessness on the part of the people in giving tithes had left the Levites destitute. Nehemiah mended that problem. He also restored the use of the Sabbath. Men, from both Israel and other nations, were trading on the Sabbath and Nehemiah reprimanded them, closing the gates prior to the Sabbath, and driving away the men who were loitering outside the gates of Jerusalem, hoping to get a jump on business after Sabbath had ended. So Nehemiah was "playing hard ball" with the people, demanding they keep covenant with Yahweh. But Nehemiah also hears the same news Ezra had heard—namely that Jews had married women from Ashdod, Ammon, and Moab. They had intermarried, showing utter disdain for God's prohibition (Deuteronomy 7:1-5). In fact, things were so bad that their children spoke the language of Ashdod and none of them could speak Hebrew. The people of God had forgotten their great God. So Nehemiah once again exhibits an intolerable burden. He tells us that he contended with them (that means he was in their faces, challenging and chastising them for their folly, like a baseball manager in the face of an umpire), he cursed them (pronounced condemnation upon them), he struck some of them, and he upped the ante from Ezra, pulling the hair out of their heads! Furthermore he made them swear by God that they would no longer give their children to be married to pagan people (Nehemiah 13:23-26).

8

Men are not sole possessors in Scripture of the intolerable burden. Hannah, the wife of the good man Elkanah who very much loved his wife, was without child and desperately wanted one. She prayed in the temple every time she was there, asking God for His favor (1 Samuel 1:3ff). She was deeply grieved over the status quo. She promised to give the child back to God, if He granted her one. We know God graciously heard her prayer and gave her a son whom she called Samuel (God hears). She, in turn, gave him to the Lord's service. Samuel became a great prophet of God, a merciful act of Yahweh in light of the wickedness and perversion of the two sons of Eli, Hophni and Phinehas.

And Anna the prophetess of Luke 2:36-38, the daughter of Phanuel, also had an intolerable burden. She was an eighty-four year old widow, whose husband had died after seven years of marriage. Luke tells us that Anna never left the temple, serving night and day with fasting and prayers. She must have prayed and fasted for over fifty years, waiting patiently and expectantly for the coming of Messiah, the Lord Jesus When she saw him she gave thanks to God and continued to speak of Him to all those who, in faith, who also were looking for the redemption of Jerusalem, for the coming of the true Savior and Lord of glory.

So, if we are to understand and engage in revival prayer then we must have a strong and solid foundation. That foundation begins first with the intolerable burden. Do you have it? Do you have an intense grief over the status quo in your own life, the church, and the world? What do I mean by the status quo in your own life? We could go many places in Scripture for the answer to this question, but perhaps the best place to look is Revelation 2,3, Jesus' letters to the seven churches of Asia Minor. Only two of these churches receive a clean bill of health from Jesus (the church at Smyrna and the church at Philadelphia). The other five are commended in various ways but also condemned as well. Take, for example, the church at Ephesus. Paul the Apostle came there at the end of his second missionary journey and then returned on his third journey, spending three years there. The church was planted around 53 A.D. We know from Acts 19 that God was working mightily in Ephesus. Demons were being cast out. Those involved in witchcraft were burning their books and fetishes, departing once and for all from them, determining to follow Jesus at all costs. And in the city where the great temple was located, the worship of Diana was suffering greatly because so many had turned from their idols to serve the true and living God. Paul wrote his letter to the church at Ephesus, while he was in a Roman prison, around 62 A.D., putting down glorious doctrine in the first three chapters, following in the last three, with a series of commands for those living in the church of Jesus. But by the time we get to the book of Revelation, written around 66 A.D.[2], Jesus tells the church at Ephesus that though they have perseverance and cannot tolerate evil men, and though they put to the test those who call themselves apostles but are not, and though they have endured for the sake of Jesus' name; He is against them because they have left their first love (Revelation 2:1-4). Think about it—in less than fifteen years this once great and mighty church is accused of leaving its first love! What

---

[2] I realize many scholars believe the Apostle John wrote Revelation around 91 A.D. but the internal evidence in the book itself seems to suggest an earlier date, probably 66 A.D., a few years before Titus of the Roman Empire invaded Jerusalem and bringing death and destruction to the city. See Gary DeMar's *Last Days Madness,* David Chilton's *Days of Vengeance*, Kenneth Gentry's *He Shall Have Dominion,* and Keith Mathison's *Postmillennialism: An Eschatology of Hope* for support of an early date of Revelation.

are the characteristics of this dynamic love they had for Jesus? They were known for their great faith in the Lord Jesus and their sincere love for the brethren (Ephesians 1:15). Paul called them God's workmanship, created in Christ Jesus for good works which God prepared beforehand for them to walk in them (Ephesians 2:10). He calls them fellow citizens with the saints, being of the household of God (Ephesians 2:19). He says they are God's beloved children (Ephesians 5:1), and that though they were formerly darkness they now have become Light in the Lord (Ephesians 5:8-9). They were zealous, hungry for Christ, committed to the work of His kingdom; but that is all gone by 66 A.D., thirteen years after the church was established.

My brethren, we must have an intolerable burden, an intense grief over the status quo in our own lives. Have you left your first love? Do you remember how it was when first Christ Jesus revealed Himself to you? If you were like me, you could not get enough of God's word. You loved good, biblical preaching. You were there every time the door to the church was opened. You attended Bible studies. You were hungry to learn all you could and you had a simple faith. If God said it, that settled it, and you obeyed it! And though you may have been rough and unpolished in your evangelistic efforts, you nonetheless, could not stop speaking about Jesus. You talked to anyone who would listen about Him. Jesus was on your lips at all times. You seemed always to get Him into every conversation. You were moved by singing the great hymns of the faith. Your sin grieved you. You lived with a constant state of awe and amazement, that your sins were forgiven, that you were declared innocent by God, given the very righteousness of Jesus. You knew you were an heir of God and a fellow heir with Jesus. You believed that God was working everything in your life for good because you loved Him.

But perhaps now you are ambivalent about preaching. You can take it or leave it. You seldom spend much more than a perfunctory time reading the word and uttering a brief prayer as you go out the door to work, preferring on your commute to listen to sports, talk radio rather than listening to gospel preaching. It used to be that you were at church Sunday morning, Sunday night, Wednesday night, and one other night during the week for Bible study or evangelistic visitation. It used to be that foul words never crossed your lips but now secretly, and perhaps sometimes very openly, your speech is tainted with cursing, lewd comments, and sexual innuendo. It may be that the thought of marital infidelity no longer repulses you, that sexual fantasies constantly plague your mind and heart. It may be that you have lowered your standards on television programming, tolerating programs you at one time would have never considered. You get the picture, don't you? Have you left your first love? If so, then repent and do the deeds which you did at first. Ask God once again to give you a hunger for His word, both in preaching and in your own personal study of it. Ask Him to make you repulsed by your sin and to give you the gift of repentance, that you no longer would grieve the Holy Spirit. Ask Him to give you a love and burden for the lost.

To go further, this intolerable burden, this intense grief over the status quo in your own personal life, is also seen in the letter to the church at Laodicea. There Jesus takes the Laodicean church to task for her lukewarmness. Not far from that city there were warm springs of water used for medicinal purposes, much like what President Franklin Roosevelt used at Warm Springs, GA to help with his polio. There also were cool springs of water people used for drinking water in that hot, arid land. But when the water from the warm springs flowed far from its source, it became lukewarm and was of no use to help with illness. And when the cool water also flowed far from its origin, it too became lukewarm and unsuitable for drinking. Both springs of water became useless, good for nothing, and ought to be vomited from one's mouth. Jesus is using this graphic language to drive home to the Laodiceans that their lukewarmness is repulsive to Him. Jesus has the same thing in mind in Matthew 5:13 when He says that we are the salt of the earth, but if the salt has become tasteless, it is good for nothing except to be thrown out and trampled under the feet of men.

Are you lukewarm, my friend? Have you grown cold toward the things of the Lord Jesus and His church? Jesus made clear that our job is to go into the whole world and to make disciples of all the nations, baptizing them in the name of the Father, the Son, and the Holy Spirit, teaching them to observe all that He has taught us (Matthew 28:18-20). Failure to do so will incur His wrath. He has eyes that are a flaming fire. His feet are like burnished bronze made to glow in a furnace. In His right hand are seven stars and out of His mouth comes a sharp two-edged sword. With it He will smite the nations. He will rule them with a rod of iron (Revelation 1:12-16, 19:11-16). He sees all we do. He calls us all to evangelize daily, to speak the truth in love daily, and to serve others daily. Are you doing so? We are to be hot with Christ. His glory ought to be on our faces, in our voices, in our eyes, moving our feet forward to a needy world. If you are not intentionally engaged in gospel work, in making disciples, in the very least praying for the progress of the gospel, contributing your money, speaking of Jesus when given opportunity with neighbors, work associates, or family members, then perhaps you have grown cold, perhaps you are lukewarm. What must you do? Jesus tells us that He disciplines those whom He loves. He tells us that He is at the door of our hearts, knocking, wishing to come in and enjoy sweet communion, as in the past. What must you do? You must open the door to the great lover of your soul. Draw near to Him and He promises to draw near again to you (James 4:7-8).

But if we are to seek God earnestly in revival prayer, if we are again to see a great and mighty movement of the Spirit, then we must also gain an intolerable burden for the church, become deeply grieved over the status quo in the church in our day. Of course, there are wonderful exceptions, but surely you will agree with me that the church in the western world is in big trouble. The materialism, the worldliness, the licentiousness, the division and strife that results in church splits is everywhere. We now have evangelical pastors and leaders who doubt the historicity of Adam and Eve, who are not so sure that homosexuality sends people to hell, who question the inerrancy of Scripture. And again, with some wonderful exceptions, much of the preaching I hear today is paltry, insipid, lacking convicting, converting, and sanctifying power. Many preachers seem content merely to give information about the Bible, believing that their job merely is to disseminate information, failing to understand what Calvin, Knox, Edwards, Whitefield, Spurgeon, and Lloyd-Jones knew so well—that true Biblical preaching is logic of fire, that while there must be light, there must also be heat, that a preacher is to afflict the comfortable and comfort the afflicted, that he must take people to Mt. Sinai before he can adequately take them to Mt. Calvary. In other words, the preacher must constantly preach the terrors of the law, not only to convict the lost of their sin to drive them to Christ; but also to preach the law to believers, driving them again to Christ for repentance and growth in grace; and he must preach the law to the world, warning everyone from the President, the Supreme Court, Congress and state and local legislators that they are not a law unto themselves, that they are accountable to the Great Judge who will judge them according to their deeds. The preacher is to be a prophet to the nations, to the universities, to Wall Street and to Main Street. He is to be a comforter to those believers wounded in conscience. He is to use the word like a hammer to shatter the pride, unbelief, and rebellion of the smug, self-righteous, and comfortable. The church is to move away from her idol of comfort and ease and venture out into the world of pain and suffering, into the inner cities where little boys and girls do not have a father at home.

If your church is not marked by earnestness in prayer, powerful gospel preaching, lots and lots of conversions, a mighty sense of the felt presence of God in your worship services, by growth in personal holiness in individuals and families, by selfless giving of time and money for kingdom expansion, by freedom and joy in everyone telling everyone they can about Jesus, by seeing the wickedness of the community dissipate, by seeing lots of men and women go into full time Christian service, and by seeing the church become a major object to be reckoned with by the enemies of Christ, then your church needs revival. You ought to gain, therefore, an intolerable burden for your church, an intense grief over the status quo.

And while this is certainly necessary personally and for the church, this intolerable burden needs also to grip us concerning our world. We could say so much here. You know the statistics. Our inner cities are in turmoil. The family everywhere is breaking down. Militant atheism is on the rise. We are losing our young people in droves, especially as they go off to college and university, unable to stand against the unbelief of Marxist college professors who poison their minds. Internet pornography is rendering millions of men intellectual zombies, enslaving them to their lusts where they prefer auto-stimulation to intercourse with their wives, robbing them of the focus they need to perform their jobs well, threatening to destroy their marriages, children, and careers. Young men are increasingly effeminate, preferring to stay at home well into their late twenties, unwilling to go out and get a productive job, unwilling to commit to marriage and rearing children. increasingly men stand on the job sidelines and the women are only too willing to take the jobs from them. I am not disparaging women at all. I don't blame them. The jobs are there for the taking, but men acquiesce, buying in unconsciously to the same old problem men have had since the fall into sin. Adam abdicated his responsibility saying to God, "The woman, whom You gave to be with me, she gave me from the tree, and I ate," (Genesis 3:12, and men have been doing it ever since. "Why work, why take on responsibility, when I can get my wife to do it!" And the last Presidential election was perhaps a tipping point in our country. Since at least the days of John Adams two world views have been at war with each other. The one believes in limited government, that the individual is responsible, without government interference, to make his way in this world. He is to work hard, to provide for his family, and he is be concerned for the poor and genuinely needy in our culture. This view acknowledges God as the One who ordains all things, including work and government. The other view, the statist position, believes the state is our savior, that we must look to the state for our sustenance. Since Woodrow Wilson, this cradle to grave outlook has been growing steadily, with the exception of eight years under President Ronald Reagan. It seems now to have overtaken us. Nearly half the people in the United States receive some sort of government assistance. This threatens to destroy our economy. We cannot continue to print money and expect our nation to prosper.

But you already know all these things, don't you? My friends, until we gain an intolerable burden, we are unable to engage in revival prayer; and without revival prayer, we will not seek God earnestly, and failure to seek God earnestly will no doubt leave us under His just condemnation. We must have revival or we are doomed.

What then, must we do? Repeatedly we find Scripture telling us that God resists the proud but gives grace to the humble, that a humble and contrite spirit, our God does not despise (James 4:10, 1 Peter 5:7, Psalm 51:17). We must see a mighty movement of God, but how? We cannot merely work ourselves up into a spiritual frenzy. We must, as Isaiah does in Isaiah 66, begin with God. Heaven is Yahweh's throne. He is transcendent and clothed with splendor and majesty. Indeed He is able to say, "I am God and there is no other, the One forming light and creating darkness, causing well being and creating calamity. I am the Lord who does all of these," (Isaiah 45:6-7). He is majestic, sovereign, holy, all powerful. Should we not tremble before the One who holds our very eternal souls in His hands! But the earth is also His footstool. God is immanent. He stoops to our weakness. He is intimately acquainted with all our ways. Even before there is a word on our tongues, the Lord knows it all. Even before you make request of your Father, He hears you. Thus you can pour out your heart to Him. He is a refuge for you. You can call upon Him in a day of trouble and He will deliver you so that you may glorify Him. Get a fresh and experiential glimpse of God's transcendence and immanence. Then ask the Holy Spirit to show you your sin, especially the sins of pride, unbelief, and rebellion.

My brethren, we are in danger of perishing as a church and nation. Without revival we are doomed. How so? Obviously I cannot predict the specifics of our doom, but it does not take much imagination to see how this may play out in the years ahead. As has happened in the Middle East, North Africa, and increasingly so in Western Europe, we could find ourselves under the dominion of Islam. We could become a third rate military and economic power and thus be more and more vulnerable to invasion by jihad. We could very well face an economic meltdown unlike anything in our history. What would happen if we had twenty-five percent unemployment? Can you imagine the rioting in the streets that could result? If we face a continued downgrade morally with the growing acceptance of same-sex marriage, then your children and grandchildren twenty years from now could be fired for putting forth the traditional and biblical view of marriage. Think of the hoopla over Chic-Fil-A's mild support of biblical marriage in July, 2012!

What are we doing? How can we continue as we are? Where is the intolerable burden? Are we not as Nero, fiddling while Rome burns? Do you not think we deserve wrath and indignation due to our contentiousness, due to our disobedience, and neglect of God's law (Romans 2:9-11)? What else can we do? Where else can we go? Should we not humble ourselves and seek God earnestly for His mercy and grace?

THE FOUNDATION FOR REVIVAL PRAYER

Chapter 2
Humiliation and Repentance

Erlo Stegen, a Lutheran pastor living in KwaZulu-Natal in South Africa, was terribly frustrated with his ministry. In the early 1960's he had been laboring among some thirty Zulu believers with little to show for his efforts. There was gross immorality, strife, and division in his little church; and the people of the surrounding villages were not at all interested in Christianity, preferring the remedies of the local witch doctor when they faced difficulty, dismissing the Christian faith as "the white man's religion." After a sermon during which Erlo said that Jesus is more powerful than the witchdoctor, a woman in the congregation asked him if that was indeed true. He said, "Of course." She said, "Then please come with me." The woman led Stegen to her small mud hut and as they entered they found the woman's daughter, naked, bound by steel wire, and tied to the center post in the hut. She had a wild and tormented look on her face. She had not eaten for days and talked incessantly in foreign languages. She was very dangerous, having bitten a man, leaving him with a bad wound on his arm. The mother had no animals left at her place, having obeyed the witch doctor who told her to sacrifice them in order to appease the ancestor spirits who were tormenting her daughter. Erlo knew immediately that the poor woman was possessed by many demons. So he and his church leaders began to pray over the woman, laying hands on her, commanding the demons in the name of Jesus to come out of her. They continued for thirty days and nothing, absolutely nothing happened!

Erlo was very discouraged and dismayed. How could this be? He began to question the authority and power of the gospel as well as the Scriptures themselves. He wondered if the gospel could indeed help such primitive people. He wondered if perhaps they were simply too ignorant, too far gone into witchcraft and animism to be helped. This led him eventually to seek God for answers. So he began gathering his little flock of Zulus for daily Bible study and prayer. They decided they would put aside their own theological systems and study the Book of Acts, asking God to show them the truth and power of the gospel. As they met daily in prayer and Bible study, God began to do a wonderful thing in Erlo Stegen's life. God began revealing to him his own sin. This was a very important revelation to Stegen because until that time, he was focusing on the sin of the Zulu people. "They were the problem. They were lazy, immoral, licentious, ignorant." Stegen began to understand that he, in fact, was the problem. God began making known to him the profound and deep seated nature of his pride. He was white. He was educated. He was cultured. He was moral. He was a good man who was sacrificing his life for these primitive people and they did not seem to appreciate his loving sacrifice on their behalf! This was an exceedingly painful and humiliating time for Erlo Stegen, but God was working on his Zulu congregation as well. They too were being broken, humbled to the dust, seeing something of the deep nature of their own pride and rebellion against God.

One day, during a worship service, while Stegen was preaching, a woman, who apparently did not understand that one does not interrupt the pastor while he is preaching, said, "Pastor, I think we should pray and ask God to make our church like the one in the Book of Acts." Stegen said, "Okay. Why don't you go ahead and pray." She prayed a simple prayer and Erlo went on with his sermon.
A week or two later, as Stegen and his congregation gathered to pray in a small house near the white people's tennis courts, Erlo was embarrassed to be seen by his white friends with these primitive black people, so he closed the door and the windows of the

14

little house so that his friends could not see or hear him praying with his church members. As they were about to pray, God seemed to speak to him saying, "If you close the doors and windows, then I am not coming in with you." So Stegen kept the door and windows open and prayed on his knees in full view of his white friends, as he and his congregation poured out their hearts to God in confession, contrition, asking for the Spirit's presence and power.

A few weeks later, while praying, this little congregation of Zulu believers and their white pastor heard and felt a mighty wind passing through their place of prayer. They knew the Holy Spirit had come upon them. As they left the place of prayer, they saw many Zulus, who had to that point utterly and completely rejected the "white man's religion", coming toward them, eager to hear the preaching of the gospel. The first convert was a witchdoctor who said that he must be saved that very moment lest he go to hell. This began in 1966 and thousands of Zulus have come to Christ over the years. Kwasizabantu means "place of shelter" in Zulu and indeed it has been that for so many. Remarkable healings, exorcisms, and conversions have continued unabated since 1966. A ten thousand seat auditorium was built many years ago to house the vast numbers who come daily to hear the preaching of God's word. A school and several farming industries also have sprung up at Kwasizabantu over the years.

By the way, the mother of the demon possessed woman whom Erlo and his leaders could not help, showed up at an evangelistic service some three years later. Stegen went again to see her. The young woman was still in her sordid state. Stegen and his leaders laid hands on her and the demons began to cry out, "We know about God and Jesus but since the Spirit has come this place is too hot for us." Some three hundred demons were cast out of this woman and immediately afterward, she had a peaceful countenance and looked as though she had been a faithful believer for many years.

If we are to see revival in our day, then we must experience profound, sincere, heartfelt humiliation for our sin, resulting in what Richard Owen Roberts calls "evangelical repentance."[3] Moral repentance is merely feeling sorry for getting caught doing something one ought not to do. It's like the man who finally asks his wife to forgive his harsh words or forgetfulness concerning her birthday, merely to gain some measure of peace in the house. Moral repentance is still a selfish act where one hopes to alleviate the tension and discomfort his actions have caused him. But evangelical repentance comes by way of the convicting and sanctifying work of the Holy Spirit, putting within the believer a holy hatred for his sin, a willingness and ability to change his actions, attitudes, and speech.

As the northern kingdom of Israel was living with the threat of Assyrian invasion, God raised up the prophet Isaiah (who preached from around 741 to 700 B.C.). He preached to both the northern kingdom of Israel and the southern kingdom of Judah, and his message was basically two-fold. First, he warned them of impending judgment due to their spiritual infidelity, going after false gods. For example, Yahweh tells them, "Bring your worthless offerings no longer. Incense is an abomination to Me . . . I cannot endure iniquity and the solemn assembly" (Isaiah 1:13). Isaiah's prophecy is full of such admonitions. And second, he sought to comfort them with the fact that He would be with them, no matter what happened (Isaiah 40:1-8, 41:10, 43:1-3). He promised them a

---

[3] For an excellent look at the Biblical doctrine of repentance I commend to you Richard Owen Roberts' book *Repentance: The First Word of the Gospel.*

redeemer who would die for them and restore them to the new heaven and earth (Isaiah 7:10-16, 9:1-7, 52:9-10, 53, 66). It is within this context that Isaiah rebukes evil leaders, calling them to repentance, promising that those who take refuge in Him will inherit the land (Isaiah 57:1-13).

And we come now to Isaiah 57:14-15 which serves as the crux of the matter concerning repentance and faith. Please consider three aspects of these two verses. In verse 14 we find Isaiah making preparation. He says, "Build up, build up, prepare the way. Remove every obstacle out of the way of My people" We find similar language in Isaiah 40:1ff where God says, "Comfort, O Comfort My people," says your God. "Speak kindly to Jerusalem, telling her that her warfare has ended, that her iniquity has been removed, that she has received of the Lord's hand double for all her sins. A voice is calling, 'Clear the way for the Lord in the wilderness; make smooth in the desert a highway for our God. Let every valley be lifted up, let every mountain and hill be made low; and the let the rough ground become a plain, and the rugged terrain a broad valley; then the glory of the Lord will be revealed, and all flesh will see it together; for the mouth of the Lord has spoken,'" (Isaiah 40:1-5). This imagery reminds me of the construction of the Interstate highway system in the United States. When building these roads, the engineers attempt to make as even a grade as possible. In other words, they want to bring down the mountains and raise up the valleys. They must remove every obstacle out of the way, all the trees, large stones, etc. so that the road can be made as level and negotiable as possible. In like manner Isaiah is commanding the people with mountainous pride to humble themselves, to be brought low; and he is telling those in the "slough of despondency and discouragement" to be built up. Another analogy is to consider landslides in mountainous regions where huge boulders or mud break loose and block highways. The roads are impassable until the state highway department brings in bulldozers and other land moving equipment to clear the way once again. God is telling the nation of Israel that they must clear all the debris from their lives, anything that hinders the free flowing work of the Spirit of God in their midst.

After the preparation mentioned in verse 14 we find next the declaration in the first part of verse 15—"For thus says the high and exalted One who lives forever, whose name is Holy. I dwell on a high and holy place, and also with the contrite and lowly of spirit." You will note here that Yahweh claims to dwell in two places. He manifests there both His transcendence and His immanence. That is, by transcendence we mean that God is holy, eternal, unchangeable. He is independent of His creation. That is, He is not helped or hindered in His personhood by anything we do or do not do. He is totally separate from all His creation. He does not exist for us, but we exist for Him. He is a consuming fire who will be no means leave the guilty unpunished. If Israel could not approach Yahweh on Mount Sinai, so we are unable to approach him either (Hebrews 12:18-21). As Moses was full of fear and trembling, so we would be too, if we came face to face with the Holy One. At the same time, however, in a most remarkable condescension, Yahweh is also immanent. That is, He is intimately acquainted with all our ways. Even before there is a word on our tongue, He knows it already (Psalm 139:1-6). We cannot flee from His presence. He is always present, always all powerful, always all knowing. He knows what we need even before we ask Him (Matthew 6:8). He hears our prayers (John 14:13-14). Therefore we are not to fear. Even though we have many afflictions the Lord, nonetheless, delivers us from them. He is near to the brokenhearted and saves those who are crushed in spirit (Psalm 34:18). You can ask Him and you will receive. You can seek Him and He will let you find Him. You can knock on the door of heaven, and He will answer you. If a son asks his father for bread, the father will not give him a stone. If a son asks a father for a fish, he certainly will not give him a snake. Arguing the lesser to

16

the greater, if we human fathers, whose lives are marked by evil or wrong doing, know how to give to our children when they ask us, then how much more should we believe that the Father in heaven will give good things to those who love Him, to those who trust Him (Matthew 7:7-11)?

But Isaiah also tells us that Yahweh dwells in one other place—the heart of the contrite and the lowly. Contrition has the idea of profound sorrow over one's sinful rebellion against God. Such a man knows he is guilty, that he deserves damnation, that he has no legal right to the blessings of the covenant of grace. Lowliness carries with it the notion of unworthiness. Such a person knows very well that if God was to mark or record his iniquities then he could never stand before Him. He knows that he is enslaved to his sin, that in him, in his flesh, no good thing dwells. He knows that, left to his own devices, he would continue the long, slow road to perdition. Nonetheless, he also knows that, by the grace of God, due to his supernatural union with Christ, he is an heir of God and a fellow heir with Christ Jesus. God is opposed to the proud but gives grace to the humble. God dwells with those who acknowledge their sin, who see their own sinful rebellion against God, who come to understand something of how they have transgressed God's law and thus brought harm to the cause of Christ and to people close to them—their spouse, children, friends, siblings, work associates, fellow church members. Ezekiel puts it in a similar fashion by saying, "Then you will remember your evil ways and your deeds which are not good, and you will loathe yourselves in your own sight for your iniquities and your abominations. . . Be ashamed and confounded for your ways, O house of Israel," (Ezekiel 36:31-32).

Thirdly, we find in the second half of verse 15 the proclamation which flows from both the declaration and preparation, "In order to revive the spirit of the lowly and to revive the heart of the contrite." Israel needed revival. They had fallen far from God's prescription for them, that they were to be His people, that He was to be their God. He promised to multiply the fruit of the tree and the produce of the field so that they would no longer receive the disgrace of famine among the nations. Instead they had profaned His holy name among the nations. Now Israel faced the coming judgment of Sennacherib and the tempestuous Assyrian army. They needed a word of comfort and encouragement. They needed to have their spirits revived and renewed, to trust their covenant God, Yahweh, who had so many times before delivered them, putting a song of praise in their hearts. Clearly, Isaiah is saying that God will revive the hearts of the contrite. He will revive the spirits of the lowly. Conversely, He will not revive those who are proud, arrogant, unbelieving, unrepentant.

We know these marvelous prophecies found their fulfillment in the first and second advents of the Lord Jesus Christ. Israel, again facing the Assyrian invasion, is comforted by the promise of a virgin conceiving and bearing a son named Immanuel (Isaiah 7:14). They were strengthened when hearing that One was coming who was the Wonderful Counselor, the Mighty God, the Everlasting Father, the Prince of Peace (Isaiah 9:6). They looked expectantly to the One who was to be pierced through for their transgressions, who was to be crushed for their iniquities, who was chastened for their well being, who bore the sins of many and who interceded for the transgressors (Isaiah 53). They rejoiced in knowing One was coming who would not break a bruised reed, who would not extinguish a dimly burning wick, who would strengthen and sustain His weak and frail people (Isaiah 42:1-3).

So, what does this all mean for us who live in a day when man continues to reject God, who puts himself defiantly in God's place, just as our forefathers did at Babel, thinking they could be like God (Genesis 3:5, 11:4)? Our history is filled with natural men (those who do not know God) who fight against Him; and supernatural men (those who are born again by the Holy Spirit) who submit to Him. It started in the Garden of Eden with Adam and Eve thinking they could know good from evil. At that point they substituted God's revelation for their own. They would carve out for themselves their own law and way of life. The result was the fall into sin and man ever since has expanded on what our first parents did. The seventeenth century Enlightenment was the more modern manifestation of this abject rebellion against God. Descartes, Hume, Voltaire, Marquis de Sade, Rousseau, Darwin, Marx, Engels, Sarte, Whitman, Emerson, and many others have put their own stamp on this rebellion but the bottom line is that man has rejected the true and living God which means he has rejected His law of God.[4] This further means that man is now free to live out his own fantasies and perversions, because in his own mind, these are completely natural. So anything goes—from homosexuality, bestiality, pedophilia, abortion, infanticide, euthanasia. You name it!

Peter tells us that judgment must begin with the household of God (1 Peter 4:17). While God certainly will judge pagan nations (Isaiah 14-20) His immediate concern is with His covenant people. I wonder if we know anything of the depth and degree of our sin against God! Richard Owen Roberts suggests that the foundation of our sin comes down to three things—pride, unbelief, and rebellion. Let's take them one at a time. First is pride. I remember preaching on this very topic a while back, mentioning in passing that while our charismatic brethren have what I called a "lousy theology" they nonetheless have faith and God blesses their faith, even though their theology is lacking. I had made that statement many times before and it never bothered me. After preaching this time, however, we were engaged in a lengthy prayer time, and God convicted me on the spot of my theological pride. I had never seen it before and it was painful to see. And then there is the problem of racial or ethnic pride, nationalistic pride. Could it be that our anger over how things are going in our country on the topic of illegal immigration, and minorities playing the "race card", has more to do with our fear of losing our ethnic and cultural place of power rather than righteousness prevailing in our nation?

Are you guilty of theological pride? Regardless of where you come down on theological issues, whether you are a Calvinist, an Arminian, a dispensationalist, a charismatic, a fundamentalist, or whatever; do you secretly think you are better than other brothers and sisters with a different theology? Do you secretly smirk when you hear others pray "shallow prayers", who listen to "dead, dry music", who are overly emotional when they worship? Fill in the blank. It doesn't matter. There is enough blame to go around for all of us. Are you guilty of political pride? Do you automatically reject anyone who votes for liberal candidates, who vote for conservative candidates? Do you place your ethnicity ahead of the gospel? While we have no doubt made progress in racial matters in the U.S., South Africa, and many other places, it seems to me that racial bigotry still is very much with us. Understand this, my friends—God resists the proud. While it is wonderfully true that if God is for us, then who can be against us (Romans 8:31), but are we sure God is always for us? Was He not against His people repeatedly in Numbers when they complained against Him, when they grumbled over Moses' leadership? God sent plagues, poisonous serpents, and earthquakes that consumed people alive; and this He did to those

---

[4] For a very good expose on modern man and where this is taking us, I recommend you read *To Be Like God: A Study of Modern Thought Since the Marquis de Sade,* R. J. Rushdoony.

whom He calls His own! Are we any better? It very well be that one of the greatest hindrances to revival in our nation, in any nation, is racial or ethnic pride.

And then consider the sin of unbelief. This manifests itself in many ways in the contemporary, evangelical church. We tend to doubt the fullness of God's attributes. We have reduced Him to a benevolent grandfather, a type of cosmic Santa Claus. We have made Him a deistic god who may have created all things, but who since that time, leaves man to his own devices, who gives man total freedom to make it on his own. This deistic god is not involved, nor is he interested in the daily affairs of anyone. Perhaps he is concerned about the really big issues of life, like the war on terror, or a tsunami that wipes out hundreds of thousands of people; but he, at the end of the day, is unable to do anything about any of it. So this deistic god will bring everyone to heaven when they die, provided they are not really, really bad people like Idi Amin, Pol Pot, or Adolf Hitler. So, people in the church doubt God's sovereignty, His absolute control over everything, that He foreordains whatsoever comes to pass. They doubt His holiness and justice, refusing to believe that He will indeed hold the guilty responsible for their sins, that He will in fact pour out His wrath on all who reject the overtures of grace made to them in the person and work of the Lord Jesus Christ.

And we also tend to doubt the authority of God's word. Forty years ago, liberals in Protestant and Roman Catholic churches were at least honest with us. They told us straightforwardly that they did not believe in the inspiration, infallibility, and inerrancy of the Scriptures. We knew where we stood with them. However today many pastors and seminary professors seem to be disingenuous. They tell us they hold to the ancient creeds of the church but their writings and preaching seems to cast a cloud over the simple belief in the authority of Scripture. We find some wanting to redefine the terms. They say they believe in the inspiration of the Scriptures, that God the Holy Spirit breathed through the writers of Scripture so that they wrote the very words of God. So far, so good. And they say they believe in the infallibility of the Scriptures, that they are true in all they teach. But then they say they are not so sure about the inerrancy of the Scriptures. Historically inerrancy has meant that the Scriptures are true in all they touch.[5] That is, if Joshua 10 says that the sun stood still for a period of time, then that is what happened. If the Scriptures say that God created the world by fiat or declaration, then that is what happened. If the Bible teaches that Adam and Eve were historical, real people, then we are not to question it. If the gospels say that Jesus healed the lame, cast out demons, raised the dead, and was Himself crucified, then that is precisely what happened. But now, some say that we cannot trust the New Testament documents, that they are in error, and that we must "pick and choose" what is authoritative and what is not.

This leads, very naturally, to unbelief concerning the preaching of God's word. The dearth of Biblical preaching in our day can be traced to our lack of confidence in the authority of the Bible. Few preachers preach with Holy Spirit unction like the great preachers of old—men like George Whitefield, Jonathan Edwards, Charles Spurgeon, James Henley Thornwell, J. Gresham Machen, or Martyn Lloyd-Jones. Consequently we are now experiencing a kind of neo-sacerdotalism where the sacrament of the Lord's Supper is preempting the preaching of the word. So, sermons are becoming shorter and shorter, less and and less powerful; and in their place we find the mystery of communion. The Reformers of the sixteenth century and the great revival preachers of the eighteenth

---

[5] *The Case for Faith,: A Journalist Investigates the Toughest Objections to Christianity,* Lee Strobel

century, while certainly embracing Baptism and the Lord's Supper, saw preaching as central to the worship service, as the primary means of grace for God's people. The preaching today seems largely to be a mere dissemination of information. We seem suspect of any preacher who shows emotion or passion when he preaches. It seems very odd to us. Our preaching generally lacks power and authority.

And because we doubt the authority of God and the Scriptures, we naturally also doubt the sufficiency of Christ. This is witnessed in many ways but I will only mention two. First, we have many within the church of Jesus who are less than fervent on holding to the exclusivity of Christ, of Jesus being the only way of salvation, as He so clearly states (John 14:6), and as His apostles proclaimed (Acts 4:12). We may hold this privately but when it comes to proclaiming it in a hostile environment, like a university setting or a community worship service with Muslims, Jews, Hindus, and Christians, then some of us are strangely silent, seemingly fearful of proclaiming the glory of Christ's propitiating, expiating, reconciling death. He alone can remove the wrath of God which we all deserve. He alone can wash away the guilt of our sin, and make us innocent before the tribunal of God's justice and holiness. He alone can make us, who were His enemies, now His friends. And second, this doubting the sufficiency of Christ makes itself known in the therapeutic gospel which is so much a part of the evangelical culture. So, we find people who are depressed, suffering from all kinds of diagnosed syndromes, and we immediately look to medication to "fix" the problem. I am not saying there is never a reason for medication, for anti-depressant medication, for example. I am saying that we tend to over medicate in our society and we also tend to look first to medication instead of the glorious power of Christ's death and the indwelling Holy Spirit to work powerfully to heal the broken-hearted, those ravaged by their own sin and the sin of others.

And finally, we seem to doubt the sufficiency of the Holy Spirit's presence and power. This, no doubt, is a product of modernity. We believe we can fix anything and everything by a seminary, a rehab project, medication, or a self-help class. So, in the church we trust our plans, programs, personalities, and projects. We pay lip service to prayer, of course, but we seem not to trust its power, its efficacy. It seems that few of us really expect anything to happen in our services, in our ministries, from our prayers. Indeed, we have not because we ask not. So our wayward sons and daughters of the church go on, wandering farther and farther from the faith. The troubled marriages in our churches continue to end in divorce and devastation to the children. Division and strife continue to rip apart one church after another. Militant atheism captures the imaginations and hearts of more and more of our young people. Those brought up in the church, schooled well in the doctrines of true Biblical faith, now question the Scripture on the homosexual issue, the exclusivity of Christ, and the eternal perdition of all who fail to embrace Christ. We tend to try many remedies to alleviate the powerlessness in our churches. We change our worship styles. We dress in different ways to "connect" with young people, to be hip and cool. We don't really believe direct, personal evangelism works anymore, that we must first makes friends with people, and then perhaps, many months or years down the road, we will have won the right to be heard by them. Some go in the other direction, shoring up a loose theological system, believing that a tighter theology guarantees church growth. We seem to try everything but the obvious. Charles Spurgeon, as he climbed the steps to the pulpit of the Metropolitan Tabernacle in London, said as each foot hit the next step, "I believe in the Holy Ghost. I believe in the Holy Ghost. I believe in the Holy Ghost." Lloyd-Jones said that while sermon preparation is vital to any preacher, he must also fervently seek the unction or anointing of the Holy Spirit upon his ministry. Again, any evangelical will of course say that he believes in the Spirit, but our actions seem to betray our confession. We spend a paltry amount of time in prayer, both personal and corporate. The unction only comes by entering the sanctuary of God (Psalm 63:1-3).

My friends, the foundation for revival, the absolutely non-negotiable elements for it are the intolerable burden and repentance and humiliation. Do you see this? Do you have an intolerable burden, an intense grief over the status quo in your own walk with Christ, in the church, and in the world? Has God begun a work of humiliation and contrition in your own heart and soul? Has this led you to repentance? Have you come to see your own pride, unbelief, and rebellion? By rebellion I simply mean an unwillingness to do the things God requires. God commands that you love Him with all your heart, soul, mind, and strength; that you love your neighbor as yourself. Do you? God also commands you not to do certain things—you are not to murder, to commit adultery, to steal, to bear false witness, to covet. To continue in these things, though we all battle with them, is to live in rebellion against the One who loves us and gave Himself up for us. Without humiliation and repentance we will not see revival.

Part II: WHAT IS REVIVAL?

Chapter 3
Revive Us Again

The small Presbyterian Church at Cambuslang, near Glasgow, Scotland, had been without a pastor for over sixteen years when young William M'Culloch arrived in 1731. The church was languishing. The new pastor found that no child under the age of sixteen in the church had been taught the *Shorter Catechism*[6], and on top of this there was a long-standing rift among several on the Session (the Board of Elders). The spiritual climate and ignorance were so pronounced, in fact, that for the first three years of his pastorate M'Culloch refused to serve the Lord's Supper. Moreover, we know that M'Culloch had serious reservations about his own suitability for pastoral ministry, for just a few years after coming to Cambuslang, he confided to an older minister that he felt totally inadequate for ministry, and in fact had run away from this church just prior to his ordination, being terrified at the prospects of such a calling.

At this time the skepticism of David Hume and the deadening effects of the Scottish Enlightenment had infected the people of Scotland, so that they were a godless, debauched people who had no fear of God before their eyes. The influence of the Puritans had faded in Scotland following the Covenanters' demise in the "killing times" at the hands of the British army in the late 1680s.[7] Thus the influence of the gospel was severely eclipsed by the late 1730s, when God raised up George Whitefield, John and Charles Wesley, Howell Harris, Daniel Rowland, and William M'Culloch to be His mighty instruments for revival in the British Isles.

Though a devout and godly man, learned and well-versed in Scripture and theology, M'Culloch was at best an average preacher, even by his own son's testimony. In fact, during the annual five-day Communion season, during which preaching continued all day long as various ministers took the pulpit, the people found M'Culloch's turn a convenient time to get up and go for a little refreshment or rest. His sermons were neither profound in content nor eloquent in delivery.

By 1740, however, M'Culloch had a deep burden for the salvation of the people of his town. He had heard of the mighty workings of God in England, Wales, and America under the preaching of George Whitefield. He had corresponded with both Whitefield and Jonathan Edwards, and been deeply moved and encouraged by their reports of the outpouring of the Holy Spirit. In 1741 he attended several of Whitefield's meetings in Glasgow, saw remarkable conversions, and was profoundly inspired by what God had done there. He wrote to Whitefield, saying that he knew of at least fifty truly converted through his preaching, ten of whom were members in M'Culloch's own church. He began to pray regularly and earnestly, searching his own heart for sin, confessing and repenting of it, being filled up regularly with the glory of Christ and the power of His gospel. He

---

[6] The *Shorter Catechism* was written by Presbyterian, Anglican, and Independent theologians at the Westminster Assembly from 1643-1647. It is part of a much larger document called the *Westminster Confession of Faith*. There is also a *Larger Catechism* included with both documents.

[7] For more information see Jock Purves' *Fair Sunshine: Character Studies on the Scottish Covenanters*.

developed a holy zeal for the lost and began to visit them regularly. He also began a prayer meeting in which a number of his elders and others from the church regularly attended. He records that his people became wonderfully given to public and private prayer, asking God earnestly for a visitation of the Holy Spirit.

Late in 1740 M'Culloch began preaching a series of sermons on the theme of the rebirth, explaining the nature of it, the necessity of it, and the means of gaining it. He spent a year plowing the fallow ground of the hearts of his cold, lethargic, ignorant people. Finally, by late 1741, his church was experiencing numerical growth with many who were awakened by the Spirit. In the early weeks of the following year, after a petition requesting regular preaching had circulated through the town and garnered many signatures, M'Culloch began preaching nearly every day. On February 18, 1742, he preached on Jeremiah 23:6, "And this is His name whereby he shall be called, the Lord our Righteousness." Nothing unusual happened during the sermon, but as he closed the meeting in prayer, perhaps due to frustration or sincere grief over the listeners' hardheartedness, M'Culloch prayed, "O Lord, who has believed our message and to whom has the arm of the Lord been revealed? Where is the fruit of my labor among this people?" Immediately the room was filled with weeping and great anguish. About fifty, wounded in their souls, went next door to the manse, and there M'Culloch spoke with each about his or her spiritual condition, praying with and for them to be granted forgiveness of their sins. For the rest of his life William M'Culloch observed the Sunday nearest February 18 as a remembrance of the great work God began that day. From February until August, a period of 120 days, there was an average of five preaching meetings weekly. The burden of daily preaching and counseling the awakened must have been a huge weight for M'Culloch to carry, but he seems to have risen to the occasion. Evidently, God gave him supernatural strength and stamina to stay at this work and God also moved a number of ministers from nearby towns to help with the counseling and preaching.

By the spring of 1742, word of the revival was spreading far and wide—word of how God was using an obscure, ordinary preacher in powerful ways. The preaching services began attracting thousands of people, and the number of those converted had grown to over three hundred. Some services attracted as many as ten thousand people. About this time M'Culloch wrote to George Whitefield, asking him to preach during the Communion season of mid July. Whitefield did preach several times. By now Whitefield had been in Scotland six months for this his second campaign there, preaching to even larger crowds than on his first visit. By the time he preached the finale of the Communion season on July 11, the crowd exceeded fifty thousand by some estimations, though Whitefield himself reckoned the count at thirty thousand. After this closing sermon Whitefield suggested to M'Culloch and his Elders that they hold another Communion season very shortly, striking while the iron was hot, so to speak, since the Holy Spirit was so obviously at work. Though it was not the custom of the Presbyterian Church to serve Communion within such a short interval, the Elders agreed and Whitefield returned on August 15 and preached to around thirty thousand again. Crowds came from nearby towns and from as far away as England and Ireland. The people were generally affected in two ways. First, many were deeply burdened by their sin, understanding their just condemnation for the first time, crying out to be saved. Others who already were in Christ were overcome with the joy of their salvation, finding their hearts wonderfully moved and energized to worship and serve God more fervently. To be sure, some mocked the proceedings, saying they were nothing but raw emotionalism orchestrated by Whitefield and M'Culloch. Others who had been opposed to the meetings, however, grudgingly admitted that those soundly converted, transformed by the preaching during the Cambuslang revival, numbered in the thousands, and that the results of the revival lasted for another thirty years. [8]

In a desire to see a mighty work of God in our day, what can we glean from the life of William M'Culloch and the Cambuslang revival? Consider these four things. *First, revival and awakening very often begin with one man who has a burden.* M'Culloch had heard of the awakening in Northampton, Massachusetts, and he had seen it with his own eyes in Glasgow. He was hungry for it in his own locale. His faith was ignited, and he was energized by the prospect of revival. M'Culloch turned his burden into fervent prayer and white-hot preaching. He gathered a number of people who prayed for revival. These prayer meetings were not forty-five minutes of sharing and fifteen minutes of prayer. The prayer times were not "organ recitals" or "travelogues." These meetings were earnest times of confession, contrition, and repentance. Some went all night, coupled with fasting. They were not haphazard gatherings but regular, consistent meetings of disciplined people who freely engaged in prayer focused on the glory of God in the salvation of sinners. Revival typically begins with one man with an intolerable burden for the glory of God. An intolerable burden is what we see in Nehemiah who, upon hearing of Judah again giving their children to be married to pagans, after all God had done in showing mercy and grace to His people; contends with them, pronouncing curses upon them, beats them, and pulls the hair out of their heads (Nehemiah 13:25).

Second, revival does not require a gifted, eloquent preacher. The Holy Spirit comes upon whom He desires, when He desires. God loves to use the foolishness of the gospel to confound the wise, the weakness of the gospel to confound the strong, that men may boast not in themselves but in God who raises the dead. The man with a burden for revival, however, wants to preach as much as possible, knowing that God's appointed means for conversion and growth in grace is the preaching of the gospel. Note also the theme of such preaching, "You must be born again." Such preaching destroys the self-confidence of the audience, stripping away the layers of self-righteousness and self-exaltation. Revival preachers must have supreme confidence in God's appointed means—preaching Christ crucified, that which exalts God and debases man. They must believe that the preacher's role is, as the Puritans used to say, to afflict the comfortable and comfort the afflicted.

Third, one who would be used of God in revival must be willing to pay the price for it; and what is that price? We see it M'Culloch's ministry. It is the total abandonment of one's right to his own schedule. M'Culloch preached almost daily, counseled with each who was awakened, and maintained his regular pastoral duties; yet we are told that he was energized by the work. He was unstoppable, tireless. Could it be that we are far too calculating in the use of our time, mapping out the hours we willingly give to ministry, not entertaining the possibility that God may require far more of us for a season? Are we willing to suffer the physical and emotional exhaustion of heaven-sent revival? Are we willing to seize the moment, if and when it comes, suspending our own hobbies and private or familial amusements for the sake of others' souls?

And fourth, the men whom God uses in revival are catholic in spirit. They are willing to work with other men, even those whose theology may be less accurate than we would

---

[8] *The Cambuslang Revival: The Scottish Evangelical Revival of the Eighteenth Century*, Arthur Fawcett, and *Scotland Saw His Glory: History of Revivals* in Scotland, compiled by Richard Owen Roberts.

like. Though M'Culloch was a Presbyterian and surrounded by Presbyterian ministers who came to assist him in the revival, he was first deeply affected by the Congregational minister Jonathan Edwards and the Anglican minister George Whitefield. Though it is clear that all three of these men held to the Calvinistic doctrines of grace and preached them uncompromisingly, it is also clear that they represented the three variations of church polity. Edwards was a Congregationalist, believing in the rule of the members of each local church. M'Culloch was a Presbyterian and thus held to Elder rule at the Sessional, Presbytery, Synod, and General Assembly levels. And Whitefield was an Anglican who embraced prelacy—the church headed by the monarch of England. Even a nominal understanding of English and Scottish history of the time recognizes a deep, abiding fracture between the two peoples, going back to Bishop Laud's cruel persecution of the Scottish Presbyterians a century earlier.[9] But men who love the gospel, who labor together for the outpouring of the Holy Spirit, put secondary issues to the side, choosing instead to focus on those matters on which they agree—the saving of souls through the preaching of the blessed gospel. Though we may not agree with others on how they worship, how they pray or preach, how they govern, if they hold to the basic creedal formulations of Nicea or Constantinople[10], then surely we ought to be able to work with them, putting aside these lesser points for the progress of the gospel and the establishing of Christ's kingdom.

So, in what area of your personal life do you need to improve? Do you have a burden for revival? Is this the ache of your soul? Do you find yourself utterly desperate for a visitation of the Spirit? Are you troubled by the worldliness, division, strife, and indifference in our churches? Do you have trouble getting people to pray diligently for revival? Do you have trouble getting people to share the gospel with the lost? Do you find that you lack boldness in one-on-one sharing of the gospel? Have you lost confidence in the simple preaching of Christ crucified to affect and change your country? Have you given up hope that God will visit us with His power? Are you ever outraged at how God's name is compromised by false worship, through false religions? Are you ever indignant at how Islam, Mormonism, and the Jehovah's Witnesses deny our blessed Lord Jesus His deity? Have you lost your vision for what God can do through you and your church? Pastor, are you physically and emotionally exhausted, ready to quit? Do you find yourself listening to that inner voice of unbelief, silently doubting, not expecting anything of significance to happen through your ministry? Are you resigned simply to take a pay check and punch the time clock until the day of your retirement, when you can play with your grandchildren all day long or gather sea shells by the sea shore? Would you say that far too often you are lazy, worldly, unbelieving, cold, hardhearted, enjoying your secret and recurring sins, giving little thought to these high and lofty ideals? Do you lack that intolerable burden of M'Culloch and Nehemiah? May God deliver you from yourself! Let us pray that God will stir us up first, then our church leaders and our people, moving us to storm the gates of heaven, beseeching God the Holy Spirit to rip open heaven and come down with great power to convict and regenerate the lost and to breathe life into our cold, worldly, complacent churches. May God so move in us that we will give Him no rest until His praise fills the earth!

But what is revival from a Biblical, exegetical perspective? What does God's word have to say about it, and what difference should this make in our churches? There is much talk

---

[9] See *The Lives of the Puritans* by Benjamin Brook, in three volumes.

[10] For details see Phillip Schaff's *Creeds of Christendom* in three volumes.

today of revival. Some see it as a series of evangelistic meetings at a church. Others see it portrayed in signs and wonders of the charismatic renewal and Neo-pentecostalism of our day. Others describe it as a renewal of the church through a sovereign act of the Holy Spirit. Some say revival is an intense time of conversion and evangelistic outreach within a church or community. I have often referred to it as the normal Christian life on steroids.

So, what do we mean by revival? From a directly Biblical and exegetical perspective, how should we define it? It appears that Psalm 85 was written after the exile, somewhere between 538 and 430 B.C., and this Psalm, along with the books of Ezra, Nehemiah, the Prophets Haggai, Zechariah, and Isaiah, and Psalm 126 serve as the Old Testament backdrop for revival. God had long warned His covenant people that idolatry would bring His judgment. He sent numerous Prophets for many years, urging both the southern and northern kingdoms to repent, to return to the Lord, and He would have mercy on them and heal their land. They refused and He sent the Assyrians in 722 B.C. to judge the northern kingdom of Israel. The southern kingdom of Judah persisted in untold rebellion and Yahweh eventually brought Nebuchadnezzar and the Babylonian empire to judge them, finally taking them into exile in 586 B.C. Daniel, a contemporary of Jeremiah, Ezekiel, and Habakkuk, while reading (Daniel 9:2) Jeremiah's prophecy about the promised return in seventy years from exile (Jeremiah 25-11-12, 29:10)—weeps, confesses, prays, and repents (Daniel 9:4ff) on behalf of God's covenant people. God graciously fulfills His promise of a return from exile by raising up Cyrus of the Medo-Persian Empire (Isaiah 45:1ff, 2 Chronicles 36:22-23, Ezra 1:1) who issues a proclamation, allowing the Jews to return to their land. They make the long trek back from what today is modern day Iraq and Iran to a place of utter devastation. The wall around the city and the temple are both destroyed. They commence to rebuild the temple but through opposition quit (Ezra 3, 4). Finally in 520 B.C., some seventeen or eighteen years after their return from exile, at the preaching of Haggai and Zechariah, the people are energized and return to their great task and complete the rebuilding of the temple.

Fast forward now another ninety years or so to 430 B.C. and Ezra comes to Jerusalem to rebuild the covenant community. He and the leaders humble themselves before the Lord and rejoice at God's goodness to them, how He protected them on their journey (Ezra 8:31ff). Ezra is then told that the Levites have not separated themselves from their pagan neighbors, that they are allowing their children to intermarry with pagans. Ezra is beside himself with grief and tears his garments, plucks out hair from his head and beard, and sits down astonished until the evening sacrifice (Ezra 9:1-4). He prays, thanking God that for a little while (since the return from exile in 538 B.C. until now, 430 B.C.) grace has come from the Lord to leave them a remnant, to give them a peg in His holy place, that God may enlighten their eyes and give them a measure of revival in the midst of their bondage (Ezra 9:8).

As was mentioned earlier, Nehemiah, a contemporary of Ezra, while living in Persia as a cupbearer to the King, hears of the wall around Jerusalem still in disrepair, after Israel has been back in the land for over one hundred years. He is grieved by this, weeps, and prays for many days, uttering an earnest prayer of repentance on behalf of God's people (Nehemiah 1:5-11). God works in the heart of King Artaxerxes, prompting him to allow Nehemiah to return to Jerusalem so that he may rebuild the wall, which he does in fifty-two days (Nehemiah 6:15). Nehemiah urges the continued return of exiles to Jerusalem and ends his book by recounting his zealous deeds on behalf of God's covenant people, telling us how he called them into account for abusing the Lord's house, for breaking the Sabbath, and for marrying pagans (Nehemiah 13:4-30). In fact, at hearing of the intermarriage with pagans Nehemiah went a step further than Ezra. He pummeled the transgressors, pronounced curses on them, and pulled out hair from their heads!

Stay with me now. I have a few more pertinent points and then I will wrap this up in a neat package. Isaiah 40-66 is a series of marvelous prophecies about the Suffering Servant, the Lord Jesus, and the glory of His coming. These are given within the context of judgment due to the idolatry of the northern and southern kingdoms. Psalm 126 is a song of praise as God's covenant people rejoice at His goodness in restoring them from their captivity. They ask the Lord to restore their captivity as the streams of the Negev (Psalm 126:4). The Negev is the desert between Judah and Egypt that is filled with scores of dry river beds that flow with powerful rushing water when the rains come to the region —an allusion to the rivers of living water promised by Jesus (Ezekiel 47, John 7:37-39).

All that I have said thus far serves as an introduction to Psalm 85, written some time after the exile. I suggest this is the model of Old Testament revival which looks forward to a great revival. So, let's take a brief look at Psalm 85 and see what it has to teach us about revival then, as well as today. The Psalm is divided into three parts. Part one, verses 1-4, deals with the *who*, proclaiming those who are the recipients of the mighty work of God in mercifully restoring people to the land after their exile. The Psalmist rejoices that Yahweh has shown favor to the land, that He has restored the captivity of His people, Jacob, that He has forgiven them their iniquity, that He has covered all their sin, that He has withdrawn His fury, and turned aside His burning anger. These are words of redemption and reconciliation. This is the little revival to which Ezra has referred (Ezra 9:8).

Part two, verses 5-9, beseech God the Lord to revive them again. It speaks of the *what* of revival. What does it look like? The Psalmist is asking God to do another great work of grace, to bring another revival—to restore them, to cause His indignation toward them to cease. He asks if Yahweh will continue His anger toward them forever, if He plans on prolonging His anger to all generations. He had earlier removed His anger, but now the Psalmist again asks Yahweh to remove it. Why? Because they have again returned to their folly! He asks God to revive His people again, that they may rejoice in Him as they had done so many countless times before (Psalm 103, 115, 126, 145-150). He concludes this section by equating revival with His lovingkindness and salvation. This is a key concept. Revival is synonymous with salvation. Revival is salvation.

And in part three, verses 9-13, the Psalmist reports the *when* of this coming great revival. He says that he waits to see what God the Lord will say. He believes that the Lord will speak peace—reconciling peace, as in regeneration, justification, and sanctification (Ezekiel 36:25-27, John 3:3-5, Romans 5:1-5, 6:1-7). He follows this wonderful hope with a strong adversative—but they are not again to return to folly. Proverbs is replete with references to the fool and his folly (Proverbs 9:6, 13:16, 14:16), to the fool who returns to his sin as a dog returns to his vomit (Proverbs 26:11), to one who refuses to heed the gracious admonitions of the Lord to walk according to the word of God (Psalm 1, Proverbs 1-6). This admonition is particularly poignant when we remember its context. God had long warned His people against idolatry and consequent judgment that would come from it. He brought judgment at the hands of the Assyrians and Babylonians. He then graciously returned them to their land. He enabled them to rebuild the wall around Jerusalem and to rebuild the Temple. They instituted the Passover and sacrificial system. Yet in their folly they returned to godlessness, giving their children to be married to pagans. The people of God are always to move forward, holding onto Yahweh the Lord through His covenant of grace, but our salvation history is filled with folly, returning again and again to false gods who lead us astray into unbelief and compromise.

But the Psalmist proceeds, telling us that this great revival will bring salvation near to all who fear Him, to all who desire more than anything God's smile, and dread more than anything His frown. This salvation, this revival, is characterized by glory that dwells in the land. The Hebrew word for *glory* connotes heaviness, awe, reverence. And what does this glory look like? In Psalm 84:11 we are told that the Lord God is a sun and shield, that He gives grace and glory. Haggai 2:7 says, "I will shake all the nations, and they will come with the wealth of all nations, and I will fill my house with glory." The prophet Zechariah says that the Lord will be a wall of fire around Zion, the people of God, that He will be the glory in their midst (Zechariah 2:7). And John tells us that the Word of God became flesh and dwelt among us, and we beheld His glory, glory as of the only begotten from the Father, full of grace and truth (John 1:14). The glory of the Lord is on the face of His people (Psalm 67:1, Numbers 6:24-26, 2 Corinthians 3:15-18). Their lives, no matter what the circumstances, reflect the glory of God in the face of Jesus. They are able to consider all things joy when they encounter trials (James 1:2-4). Though afflicted they are not crushed, though perplexed they are not despairing, though persecuted they are not forsaken, though struck down, they are not destroyed. They are always carrying in their bodies the dying of Jesus so that in them may be seen the living of Jesus (2 Corinthians 4:7-10).

The Psalmist goes further. He says that the great revival will bring a remarkable reconciling grace to the covenant community. God's lovingkindness, that is His love, mercy, and grace will meet His truth. John says that grace and truth were realized through Jesus Christ (John 1:17). The judgment our sin deserves, the very truth about all of us, is met in the grace of God through the coming Messiah. Righteousness (the demands of the Law which reveal the very character of God) and peace (right standing with God, our estrangement, having been removed) have kissed each other. David tells us to kiss the Son, to do homage to the Son, lest He become angry and we perish in the way. For His wrath waits to be kindled and without kissing Him we surely would perish eternally (Psalm 2:12). The Psalmist continues His evidences of the great future revival, telling us that truth will spring up from the earth. Isaiah prophesies a similar glory—telling us that the heavens will drip down from above, that the clouds will pour down righteousness, that the earth will open up and salvation will bear fruit, that righteousness will spring up with it (Isaiah 45:8). Surely this is language of great abundance! God is promising a better day, a day when the glory of the Lord will cover the earth as the waters cover the sea (Habakkuk 2:14). He concludes the Psalm by proclaiming a day of wonderful prosperity, telling us that Yahweh the Lord will give what is good (Psalm 145:14-21), that our land will yield its produce. This is revival language, pointing to a spiritual application in the salvation of the nations (Psalm 126:4-6, Zechariah 2:11, 6:12, 8:22, 9:16, 10:12, 12:10, 13:9, 14:9). He prophesies that the great revival will bring Messiah, His very righteousness and holiness going before Him, preparing the way of the Lord (Isaiah 40:1-5, Malachi 3:1-4).

One question remains—what is the great revival and when does it occur? If we understand that revival and salvation are synonymous, that glory is to dwell in the land, if this is a long awaited prophecy, then surely we can discern that the great revival occurred on the day of Pentecost when the promised Holy Spirit came, when Peter preached with such power and three thousand were saved in one day. All the marks of revival, seen in Psalm 85, within the context of Ezra, Nehemiah, Daniel, Isaiah, Haggai, and Zechariah, are present at Pentecost, as reported in Acts 2, and in the succeeding chapters of the Acts of the Apostles. In other words, revival is salvation. Revival is glory dwelling in a land, in a church. Revival is what we see in the books of Acts, what we see prophesied in Psalm 85. It is what Ezra, Nehemiah, Daniel, and Zechariah all longed to see. They rejoiced in the little revival but they waited earnestly for the great revival. Revival is mighty praying, mighty preaching, mighty conversions, mighty assemblies, mighty gospel holiness, mighty generosity, mighty personal evangelism, mighty societal impact, mighty leadership, and mighty opposition.

And here is this very, very encouraging thing—we can have revival. God wants to bring it! He wants the church to regain her glory found in the book of Acts. I am not speaking of three easy steps like what Charles Finney believed.[11] Brian Edwards has noted that Finney said one fact under the government of God of universal note is that the most useful and important things are most easily and certainly obtained by the use of the appropriate means. But neither am I speaking of what so many today teach, that we ought to seek God for revival, but we have no guarantee that He will ever bring it.[12] It is clear from Scripture that revival is the norm, that we do not have revival because we have returned to folly, because we have returned to trusting ourselves, because we embrace worldliness, because we fail to pray and repent, because we are in bed with spiritual harlotry. If we would draw near to God, then He promises to draw near to us (James 4:8). He will allow us to find Him if we seek Him will all our heart (Isaiah 65:1-2). The question is—are you willing to pay the price to regain the revival culture of Acts, of that which has been so much a part of our history? What will you do with what you now know?

---

[11] See *Can We Pray for Revival?* By Brian Edwards, page 16.

[12] See Martyn Lloyd-Jones in his book *Revival.*

Part II: WHAT IS REVIVAL?

Chapter 4
Revivals in Church History

The 1949 revival on the Isle of Lewis, off the western coast of Scotland in the Hebrides was glorious and powerful.[13] It is thrilling to read of what happened there. Before we look at this revival and other revivals in more detail; we first need a geography and history lesson. The Isle of Lewis is an island, sixty miles long, facing the gale winds of the northern Atlantic Ocean, a very difficult and unpleasant place to live. It is cold, windy, snowy in winter and barren with few trees. Only 25,000 people live there, mainly in small communities near the coast. The largest city is Stornoway with only 10,000 people. Most are small time farmers working their six acre plots which they call crofts. A large portion of the men sail the world as merchant marines. At the time of the 1949 revival travel back to the mainland by boat took eight hours. So it is clear that the Isle of Lewis was very isolated. The southern part of the island is called Harris, from where we get the famous Harris tweed.

The people, even to this day, are God-fearing people, though this was not always the case. The gospel did not come to Lewis until portions of the Bible were translated into Gaelic in 1767. It was not until 1800 that the whole Bible was available in the Gaelic language, and in 1820, through the preaching of Alexander MacLeod at the town of Barvis, revival came, bringing great conviction of sin and salvation to thousands of people. From that time nearly the entire population of Lewis attended church every Sunday and honored the Lord's Day by refusing to do any work on that day. Men, believer and unbeliever alike, held morning and evening family devotional times, reading the Scriptures and the *Shorter Catechism* of the *Westminster Confession of Faith*, closing their times with a prayer. They believed this was their covenant responsibility, though many were not true believers. Crime and drunkenness were almost non-existent, and many of the towns had only one policeman who merely handled paperwork in the town. People routinely left their peat (used for fuel) on the side of the road to dry and no one would dream of stealing it. The same was true with goods the people were selling.

The only churches on Lewis were Presbyterian. The Presbyterian Church of Scotland, that is the national church, the Free Church of Scotland, and the small and separatist Free Presbyterian Church of Scotland were the churches at which the people worshipped. All three denominations were faithful to the Scriptures though the national church on the mainland was quite liberal theologically by the time of the revival. The Great Disruption of 1843 brought division, producing the national and free churches. At the time of the 1949 revival there was a great deal of distrust between the various denominations. In fact it is interesting to note that the revival came though the liberal denomination, the Presbyterian Church of Scotland. This immediately caused the conservative Free Church of Scotland to be suspect of it, urging their congregants not to attend the meetings. Again, it is important to remember that on Lewis even the national church was theologically conservative.

Prayer was central to this revival, as it is in any revival. All the true believers would gather for a mid week prayer meeting. Those who attended Sunday worship, but who

---

[13] *Sounds from Heaven: The Revival on the Isle of Lewis, 1949-1952*, Colin and Mary Peckham

were not yet converted, did not attend the prayer meetings. In fact it was seen as a major step of faith when one began attending these prayer meetings. Open prayer was not done. The pastor would ask three or four men to lead in prayer, and when the Holy Spirit came upon them, the prayer meetings were endued with a remarkable sense of God's presence.

Neither women nor children were allowed to pray, though they attended. The people were thorough going Calvinists, believing in all our distinctive doctrines—the infallibility and inerrancy of Scripture, the depravity of man, the imputation of Adam's sin, the sovereign and electing grace of God, the utter sufficiency of Christ for salvation, and the sheer grace of God in granting it. Other than in the town of Stornoway, the people at the time exclusively spoke Gaelic and all the revival work was done in that language. The people sang Psalms from the Scottish Psalter with no instrumentation, and those present during the revival spoke of the incredible energy and beauty of the singing. Finally, the Isle of Lewis had a long history of revivals. I have already mentioned the 1820 revival but the 1859 and 1904 revivals in America, Wales, England, and Scotland also swept over Lewis. However, Lewis also experienced a very powerful revival in 1939, which whet the appetite of the people for what happened in 1949. Contrary to what has been extensively reported, the 1949 revival on Lewis did not start with two little old ladies praying. These two ladies, the Smith sisters, did in fact pray regularly for revival, but hundreds of other believers were praying too.

The man whom God used in the 1949 Lewis revival was the Reverend Duncan Campbell, of the Presbyterian Church of Scotland. Campbell had been used powerfully ten years before in the 1939 revival but had settled into a local pastorate. Little power was manifested in his pastoral ministry and he was terribly perplexed by this. On one occasion his young daughter asked him, "Father, why are you not seeing revival in your ministry any longer?" Shortly thereafter, he unmistakably sensed God's calling to give up his pastoral ministry and begin an itinerant preaching ministry under the auspices of the Faith Mission. He began by preaching at Barvis, on the Isle of Lewis, on December 7, 1949, at the local Presbyterian Church of Scotland congregation. He says that he preached to a crowded church, the service beginning at 7 p.m. and not ending until 10:45 p.m. A number of people were under deep conviction of sin and he urged them to come sit before the pulpit and he and the pastor did their best to lead them to Christ. It is important to note that Campbell never "led anyone in a prayer to receive Christ." Instead he gave them promises from God's word and urged them to seek God until He gave them peace. Over the next two weeks meetings were held nightly where he preached the terrors of the law and the awful reality of hell for all the lost. He then came in with the balm of Gilead, urging people to come to the beautiful Savior. Many gathered in after meetings at various homes in the community. Believers and seekers, those under deep conviction of sin, would pray and sing Psalms, as well as listen to another sermon by Campbell. These meetings routinely went until 3 a.m., sometimes going all night. Through August, 1952 Campbell routinely preached two to three week meetings in most of the towns of Lewis, usually taking a week break for rest between them. Some accused Duncan Campbell of being an Arminian, but he steadfastly denied the accusation. He said that he believed in election but he also believed that election would not override anyone's coming to Christ.

Campbell was routinely given a special word from God which awed the people. On one occasion some coming to the meeting were delayed through the breakdown of the bus on which they were traveling. They finally made it, coming by boat. Campbell, not knowing anything of the circumstances, stood to preach from John 6:24, "They themselves got into small boats and came to Capernaum, seeking Jesus." Mary Peckham, who was a most reluctant and hard hearted teenager at the time, came to one meeting with four of her girl friends. As they approached the church Mary told them that she believed Campbell would preach on the five virgins from Matthew 25, and he did just that. Sometime after this, while under deep conviction of sin, Mary was reading her Bible daily but she was also reading *The People's Friend*, a worldly magazine. At one meeting Mary and her cousin heard Campbell say, looking directly at them, "Some of you here have the Bible in one hand and *The People's Friend* in another." Obviously they were awed by this.

We need briefly to understand something of the characteristics of the Lewis revival. First, it was driven by the preaching of the word of God. The 1904 Welsh revival and the 1939 Lewis revivals were driven by prayer, and though powerful, were short lived. Duncan Campbell preached from Genesis to Revelation on all the great themes of the Bible, stressing their disobedience to the Law of God and their consequent judgment, painting vivid pictures of the horror of hell; and then preaching the beauty and excellency of Christ. The people felt as though Campbell was speaking directly to them, that he knew all about their sin. He was very bold in the pulpit but very gentle and patient when dealing individually with seekers. Second, the revival was fueled by prayer, lots of prayer. There was unity and expectancy in prayer. Hundreds of people across Lewis were praying in small groups, for hours at a time, urging God to pour out His Spirit upon them. The after meetings during the revival largely were prayer meetings, sometimes lasting all night. When the Spirit was bringing conviction and conversion the people prayed, wondering who it would be that night, who would be saved in the meeting. The day after these meetings would find the postman going from house to house, delivering the mail, giving people news of who was converted the night before. Third, the singing of Psalms was heavenly. Those who heard the singing were awed by it, saying there was nothing like revival singing. They said it seemed supernatural, full of joy, and spiritual power. The people sang everywhere- in their homes, on their jobs, on the public buses. Fourth, there was great joy, boldness, and unity in the revival. The divisions between the churches, while still present among the ministers, were broken down among the people during the revival. People routinely attended other churches and fellowshipped with brethren from those churches which they previously would have neglected. Fifth, there was a deep hunger for the things of God. The revival completely consumed the people and the use of their spare time. The people packed into the churches and many remained outside to hear when they could not enter. A majority of the people would move to homes for the after meetings which lasted until after midnight or even later. The people drank up the word of God with insatiable thirst. Campbell was swamped with invitations to preach all over Lewis and Harris.

The greatest characteristic of the revival, however, was the felt presence of God. All the witnesses to the revival in Lewis spoke of it. They referred to an overwhelming sense of awe, reverence, conviction of sin. Some had unutterable joy, especially after they were converted, while prior to their conversion there was great misery, anxiety, and fear for their lost condition. The preaching of Duncan Campbell was also attended with a powerful sense of God's presence. The people believed that God was dealing directly with their souls. Christ was made to be very real to them. He no longer remained a distant, theological concept. The sense of God's presence came to thousands who gained a deep love for Christ and a consequent peace and joy.

This powerful sense of God's presence also made itself known in strong impressions or leadings from God, things which later confirmed God's initiation of them. On one occasion Duncan Campbell was on the platform of an evangelistic meeting in Bangor, Northern Ireland and was to preach there the following evening. While on the platform he had a very strong impression that he must leave the meeting and immediately travel to Berneray on the Isle of Harris. He did so and when arriving there was told that a layman, Hector MacKinnon, had prayed at the exact time Campbell was moved to come to Lewis, asking God to send Campbell to them for a harvest of souls. There also were strange physical manifestations of God's presence. Some were given gifts to write poetry and set their poems to music. These were people who had never written poems or composed music. Many of these Gaelic hymns were sung for years afterward. Others reported being in a home meeting, crowded with people one evening, feeling the house move. Others said they heard heavenly music. These sorts of things seem strange to Presbyterians, like me, but I remind you that the people of Lewis were all Presbyterians. They believed in and experienced what theologians call "the immediacy of the Holy Spirit." This was not abstract, ivory tower theology, but experiential, immediate visitations and manifestations of the Spirit.

However church history, just in the last four hundred years, is replete with example after example of heaven sent revival. In 1590, after the great work of God under John Knox's leadership in Scotland was on the wane, John Davidson, a young Presbyterian pastor in the Church of Scotland, was deeply burdened for the cold, lifeless way that so many of the ministers of his day went about their ministries. He called the General Assembly of the Church of Scotland to repent and pray for revival. They did so, and God brought deep conviction of sin, resulting in repentance, and a renewed resolve to preach Christ crucified in their churches. Consider then the preaching at Kirk o'Shotts in the summer of 1630 by John Livingstone as another case in point. [14] Livingstone was a young man, not yet ordained into the Presbyterian ministry, who was asked to preach the last service, on Monday, at the seasonal communion service. On Monday morning he went out into the fields to pray and meditate on his sermon, and the longer he did so, the more and more fearful he became. He finally decided that he could stand and preach before such a large crowd. He turned away from the village, and was fleeing as people were coming toward him to the meeting. Conviction of sin overcame Livingstone. He obeyed God, and preached powerfully from Ezekiel 36:25-27 on regeneration, justification, and sanctification. After preaching for one hour, he came to the application of his sermon and preached another hour. The Holy Spirit fell with convicting and converting power. At least five hundred of the five thousand present marked that day as the one in which they came from death to life.

The Reformation of the sixteenth century with Martin Luther, John Calvin, and John Knox was nothing less than a mighty movement of God, a heaven sent revival. Both Germany and Scotland were transformed by it. The city of Geneva, under Calvin's preaching and writing ministry, was deeply impacted by it, becoming the most Christianized place on the earth at the time. So too was the Puritan revolution of the seventeenth century a revival of true religion, giving us such powerful preachers as Cotton and Increase Mather, Thomas Hooker, John Owen, John Flavel, Joseph Alleine, Thomas Brooks and many, many others. Under John Winthrop's able leadership, as he put forth the American "city on a hill" vision, the Massachusetts Bay Colony was established as a God-fearing community. Within eight years of their arrival in 1630 the Puritans had established Harvard University to train men for the gospel ministry. Historians have also acknowledged that the seventeenth century Dutch, in making a covenant with God, largely attributed their wealth and power to God and the Reformation

---

[14] For more details on both Davidson and Livingston's part in these revivals, see *They Saw Scotland's Glory,* Richard Owen Roberts.

principles they were instituting in their culture. [15]And then the Great Awakening in America, Scotland, Wales, and England was a mighty revival of unprecedented proportions. Jonathan Edwards, from January to June, 1735 said between ten and fifteen people weekly were converted. One observer wondered if the whole town of Northampton, Massachusetts, where Edwards lived and preached, had been converted. George Whitefield, a contemporary and friend of Edwards', crossed the Atlanta Ocean thirteen times, preaching up and down the Atlantic seaboard, as well as in the open fields of England, Scotland, and Wales, sometimes to as many as fifty thousand people at one time. It has been estimated that at least ten percent of the population of three hundred thousand in New England in 1740, some thirty thousand people, were converted during this period. There is little doubt that the Great Awakening in the American colonies was a catalyst leading to the American Revolution. The people, converted between 1735 and 1765, having also imbibed of the teaching of Samuel Rutherford in Lex Rex[16], were longing for freedom. Historians have rightly observed the difference between the godless, vile, and wicked French Revolution and the relatively bloodless American Revolution, saying the former was fueled by the skepticism of Rousseau and Hume; while the latter was energized by Calvin, Knox, and Rutherford.

Then there was also what some call the "Hidden Revival"[17] in England and Scotland from 1790 to 1840 which resulted in nearly two million conversions. It was called a hidden revival because so little is written about it. It was eclipsed by the more widely known Great Awakening which preceded it and the Second Great Awakening which followed it in America. And when we move into the nineteenth century we see another great and mighty movement of God in America, the Second Great Awakening, from around 1800 to 1840. During this time God raised up mighty preachers like Asahel Nettleton, Charles Finney, and James Brainerd Taylor. While there were certainly unbiblical aspects to this revival[18], it resulted in thousands of conversions in America at the time. While part of the motivation for the abolition of slavery in America was Jacobin (atheistic, inspired by the skepticism of the French Revolution), it is also true that in the north, many believers, as a result of the revival, where ardently for the abolition of slavery and labored incessantly for it.

And at the height of an economic recession in America in 1858 when hundreds on Wall Street were losing their wealth, Jeremiah Lamphier called for daily prayer for revival in New York City. Within a few weeks thousands of businessmen were taking their lunch hour to gather in the churches of Manhattan to repent and pray for revival. The revival spread throughout the United States, making its way to Northern Ireland and Wales as well. The revival continued during the American War Between the States, resulting in

---

[15] See *The Embarrassment of Riches: An Interpretation of Dutch Culture in the Golden Age,* by Simon Schama

[16] See my devotional entitled "May Christians Engage in Civil Disobedience," November 15, 2012, archived at <www.pefministry.org> for a fuller explanation of this issue.

[17] From *Give Him No Rest,* Erroll Hulse, pages 97-100.

[18] For an excellent examination of this issue I commend to you Iain Murray's book *Revival and Revivalism: The Making and Marring of American Evangelicalism, 1750-1838.*

thousands of conversions in the armies of the Confederacy.[19] Beyond this, we find young Evan Roberts of Wales, asking permission from his Bible College president to return to his home church and deliver a message "from God." Roberts, having been granted permission, showed up on a Wednesday night service, asking the pastor for the privilege to speak to the congregation. After the service a few people, mainly teenagers, remained behind. Roberts challenged them to repent of any known sin, to refrain from anything which is questionable, to confess Christ publicly, and to obey the Spirit's promptings immediately. This small group of young believers began praying, weeping, confessing their sins, and the Spirit came upon them. Very quickly this prayer revival spread throughout the south of Wales, eventually ushering thousands into the kingdom of God. James Orr has observed how the very fabric of the Welsh community was drastically altered through this revival.[20] Drinking establishments went out of business. The ponies, which transported coal from the mines, refused to work after the revival. The reason? The men who worked with the ponies, prior to conversion, swore incessantly at them to get them to work. But since the men no longer swore, the ponies did not know what to do! Policemen had little to do and so offered to sing at the revival meetings. And while we have not had a major revival or awakening in the western world (there have been several small revivals, like at Wheaton College and Asbury College in the early 1970's) in over one hundred years, there are plenty of them today in places like China and India. The church in China now numbers at least one hundred million. If conversions continue, among the untouchables of India, the so-called Dalits, then some estimate that India will be a Christian nation within fifty years! A great revival has been running, uninterrupted for over fifty years in East African countries like Uganda, Malawi, and Kenya. I have seen, first hand, the remarkable interest in God's word. The people routinely sit all day on uncomfortable benches just to hear the preached word of God.

So while the 1949 revival on the Isle of Lewis, and the others like them, just mentioned, are wonderfully encouraging to me it also causes me great concern for our day. How so? When surveying the great movements of God in the western world, the 1949 Isle of Lewis revival is the last revival, over fifty years ago. The mighty movements of God today are occurring in developing nations like China, India, and many African countries. What is the one common denominator in all of them? The people have few distractions. They are relatively poor and lack options for an easier life. The people of Lewis were almost completely cut off from the rest of the world. Tourists almost never came there. The people had lived there for hundreds of years, never moving from their villages. Almost none had automobiles or any modern conveniences. The limited distractions enabled them to focus on their crofts, weaving Harris tweed, and having morning and evening family devotional times, attending weekly prayer meetings, and giving their entire Sundays to Lord's Day observances. They did not have to choose between attending the prayer meeting or their children's sports or school activities. They did not have to choose between attending church or Sunday professional sports venues for they did not exist. They did not have television and so were not distracted from gospel endeavors by watching *American Idol* or some equivalent. Their limited access to the world wonderfully sheltered them from things which could steal their heart for lesser things.

---

[19] See T*he Great Revival in the Southern Armies,* published by Sprinkle Publications.

[20] *Wales Revival—The Awakening of 1904 in Wales,* J. Edwin Orr

Our problem, which I fear will hinder our serious pursuit of revival, is the curse of modernity. We have such wealth, such ease of life, such easy access to illimitable forms of recreation that these mitigate any zeal for revival which we may develop. While recently reading *The Sounds of Heaven* on a plane I was deeply moved and was contemplating what this could mean for ministry in today's world. While being caught up in the glory of the revival on Lewis, I happened to look through two seats in front of me and saw a man watching a DVD on his computer. I could not hear anything nor did the movie appear to be that compelling. Nevertheless I found myself looking at it, intrigued by it, distracted from a much more heavenly pursuit by a movie of little consequence.

Or consider this example. In the late 1950's, through the early 1970's *Presbyterian Evangelistic Fellowship* (PEF) revival and evangelistic preachers, men like Bill Hill, Arnie Maves, Sam Patterson, and at least nine more, regularly conducted eight day meetings in churches. They typically came to a town on a Saturday and sometimes preached that night. But they always then preached Sunday morning and Sunday night, conducted morning Bible studies, and preached each night through to the next Sunday night, and the churches were full. Usually by Wednesday or Thursday night, the Holy Spirit would break the unregenerate hearts of those present and many were converted then and over the succeeding nights. Sometimes the meetings lasted for thirty straight nights! Now, what do you think would happen if I, or some other evangelistic preacher, was willing to preach in a local church, but required all to attend, morning and evening for eight straight days! Impossible! Few would agree to it. Even fewer would attend. Why? Is it because people are altogether uninterested in the gospel? Not necessarily. It is simply because we have so many other options. The good has become the enemy of the great. We have all manner of entertainment to keep us occupied at night. We have our children's sports, dance, and music commitments which take up their afternoons, bleeding over into the evening, crowding out family time, let alone the possibility of coming nightly to church to hear the preaching of the gospel. We travel so much in our jobs and the demand of immediate access through iPhones makes it exceedingly difficult for most of us to disengage and consider the need of our eternal souls.

Do these not illustrate our dilemma? We can be earnest for revival, saying that we will dedicate long hours to prayer and meditation, encouraging our church people to do the same, practicing self-examination, crying out to God to rend the heavens and come down with an awesome display of His felt presence. At the end of the day, however, we are so easily distracted by the curse of modernity. We have our smart phones, iPads, computers and the internet, and unlimited access to every form of entertainment imaginable and these distract us from our heavenly calling.

I was speaking some time ago with a pastor serving a congregation on the Gulf Coast of the United States, and he told me that they were seeing a number of remarkable conversions of people who previously were hostile to the gospel or had no interest in it. When I asked what he considered the human reason for these conversions, he said clearly Hurricane Katrina was at work. The people had been stripped of everything. They were desperate and had few options. They had no entertainment. They had time on their hands. They had time to consider the needs of their eternal souls.

Here's the main point of what I am saying- ***could it be that God will not bring revival until we are serious about pursuing Him for it, and could it be that we will not be serious until we are stripped of everything?*** If my premise is correct then the question remains—are we willing to pay the price for revival? After all, we have our own salvation. Why should we be so concerned about the souls of others? I fear we lack a zeal for the glory of God, for the felt presence of God which strips man of his self-confidence. Are we willing to say to God, "Do whatever it takes in my life, in our nation, bring whatever catastrophe You must to strip away our options for frivolity." Are we willing to have God remove the curse of modernity, if it would bring revival?

Part II: WHAT IS REVIVAL?

Chapter 5
The Ten Marks of a Revival Culture

David Brainerd was born in April, 1718 in Haddam, Connecticut and was converted just prior to enrolling at Yale in September, 1739. He was deeply and profoundly affected by the preaching of George Whitefield at Yale in the fall of 1741 at the height of a remarkable visitation of the Holy Spirit in New England. Later that fall Whitefield joined Jonathan Edwards at his church in Northampton, Massachusetts where there was a steady stream of conversions. Brainerd was dismissed from Yale due to harsh things he said about a tutor, saying off handedly that the tutor had no more grace than a chair. He sought to be reinstated but to no avail. He began his missionary work in November, 1742 among the Indians of the Kaunaumeek tribe, who resided halfway between Stockbridge, Massachusetts and Albany, New York. He saw little fruit from his efforts. At this juncture, Brainerd's circumstances—extreme physical deprivation of hunger, illness, and isolation, coupled with a deep conviction of his own sin and unworthiness—drove him to prayer. He spent long hours in the woods, in isolation, pouring out his heart to God in prayer, confessing his sin, delighting in the glory of Christ and the grace of the gospel, beseeching God for the salvation of the poor, heathen Indians. He traveled in the spring of 1744 to the forks of the Delaware River in Pennsylvania and again saw little openness to the gospel among these pagan and primitive people. Many had been hardened by white men who called themselves Christians but who lived godless, debauched lives. However in the summer of 1745 at Crossweeksung in New Jersey, Brainerd began to find the Indian tribe there melted by his and William Tennent's preaching. Brainerd and Tennent found among the Indians a quiet weeping and sobbing, a profound awareness of their sin. They believed this to be an earnest desire to be saved. Brainerd, through his interpreter, went from house to house, daily preaching Jesus; and he continued also daily with public meetings where he proclaimed the simple message of the cross, calling them to flee to Jesus to be saved. Indians from as far as forty miles were coming to the meetings, falling under conviction of their sin, and calling on Christ to be saved. Brainerd never mentions how many he thinks were converted but by noting his references to how many attended various meetings, it seems safe to say that several hundred were wonderfully born again during August, 1745. These conversions continued unabated into the next year.[21]

Later Brainerd writes in his diary of the societal impact conversion had on the Indians of Crossweeksung. He says,

"The effects of this work have likewise been very remarkable. I doubt not that many of these people have gained more doctrinal knowledge of divine truths since I first visited them in June last, than could have been instilled into their minds by the most diligent use of proper and instructive means for whole years together, without such a divine influence. . . Their pagan notions and idolatrous practices seem to be entirely abandoned in these parts. . . They seem generally divorced from drunkenness, their darling vice, the "sin that easily besets them," so that I do not know more than two or three, who have been my steady hearers, that have drank to excess since I first visited them . . . As their sorrows under convictions have been great and pressing, so many of them have since appeared to "rejoice with joy unspeakable, and full of glory," and yet I never saw anything ecstatic or flighty in their joy. . . some of them have been surprised at

---

[21] *The Life of David Brainerd*, compiled by Jonathan Edwards, pages 144ff.

themselves, and have with concern observed to me, that "when their hearts have been glad," which is a phrase they commonly make use of to express spiritual joy, "they could not help crying for all."[22]

Is the Book of Acts a mere aberration or is it to be the benchmark, the gold standard, as it were, of Christianity? What should characterize the church in our day, in any time of history? James Boice says that the church today rarely understands the far reaching impact of the early church, how they had taken the gospel to the farthest reaches of the Roman Empire, if not further, within two hundred years of Pentecost.[23] Acts is the fulfillment of Old Testament prophecy where the promised Holy Spirit was to come upon the covenant community and empower her to fulfill the Great Commission of our Lord.[24] I suggest the Acts of the Apostles is normative for the church in any age. I am not speaking of tongues and miracles. These are not the focus of Luke's writing. The unmistakable theme is the expansion of the gospel to Jerusalem, Judea, Samaria, and the uttermost parts of the earth, (Acts 1:8). If the Holy Spirit enabled that kind of kingdom expansion then, should this not be the same in our day, in any day, in any nation?

So, what characterized the church in Acts and what ought to characterize us today? What would revival look like in our day? I see at least ten marks of revival present in Acts, and there is, I suggest, an order to them. One cannot miss these marks in the ministry of David Brainerd, as noted briefly above. First, in the Acts of the Apostles, there is clear evidence of mighty prayer. The one hundred and twenty were gathered together in the upper room for ten days of prayer, after Jesus' ascension (Acts 1:12-14). For what were they praying? No doubt they were praising God for the death, resurrection, and ascension of the Lord Jesus. Surely they were giving thanks to God for opening their eyes to see the truth as it is in Jesus. Can there be little doubt that they were also confessing sin, being reconciled to one another. No doubt they each had sin to confess in denying Jesus and losing track of His demands on their lives. Foremost, however, these saints were praying for the promised Holy Spirit. Jesus had told them to proclaim repentance for the forgiveness of sins and to remain in the city until they were clothed with power from on high (Luke 24:47-49). He also told them, just prior to His ascension, that they would receive power when the Holy Spirit came upon them, that they then were to be His witnesses (Acts 1:8). And when Peter preached at Pentecost, a few days after their prayer in the upper room, he reminded his hearers that the outpouring of the Holy Spirit, which they were witnessing, was a fulfillment of Joel's prophecy, that the Holy Spirit was to be poured out on all flesh, on all mankind (Joel 2:28-29). So, they were asking for the promised Spirit to come upon them in order to empower them for His Great Commission. They were asking for Holy Ghost power! Mighty prayer, as seen in the prayers of Ezra (Ezra 9:5ff), Nehemiah (1:4ff, 9:5ff), and Daniel (9:4ff) is always characterized by an intolerable burden for the glory of God to dwell in the land (Psalm 85:9), for Jesus to be a light to the nations (Isaiah 49:6), for God's face to shine on His people (Psalm 67:1), for multitudes to taste of Christ's fullness (John 1:16). Mighty prayer induces an indomitable hunger for Christ, getting to the place where we can say with the Psalmist, "Whom have I in heaven but Thee? And besides Thee, I desire nothing on earth, (Psalm 73:25). Mighty prayer is marked by faith, fervency, urgency, humility, and persistence. In mighty prayer,

---

[22] Ibid, pages 190-191.

[23] *Acts: An Expositional Commentary*, Boice, page 22.

[24] See Joel 2:28-29 Ezra 9:8-9 (a little reviving), Luke 24:49, John 14:16-17, 16:5-11, Acts 1:8.

one has a deep sense—like the Syrophonecian woman (Mark 7:24-30), whose daughter was demon possessed—of coming to Jesus with desperation, humiliation, and hope. She had tried everything to help her daughter but nothing had worked. She heard of Jesus, and believed He could help her daughter. So she went to Him expectantly. But he immediately rebuked her, reminding her that a Jew is not to give food to a dog, a Gentile. He put her down, not because He despised her, but to show the contrast between Him and the religious leaders of Israel. To them, the unbeliever, the Gentile, was a dog, but to Jesus she/they were potential recipients of His grace. She persisted, telling Jesus that even the dogs ought to be able to eat crumbs from the master's table. God rewarded her great faith by healing her daughter. Like this woman, we must come humbly, expectantly, persistently, unashamedly, not giving God rest until He once again exalts His name as a praise among the nations of the earth. Do you pray mightily in the Spirit? I will detail later what I mean by mighty praying, but for now, please understand that this is the first foundational and essential characteristic of every revival culture.

Second, mighty prayer always leads to mighty preaching—what we may also call revival preaching. This is clearly present in the books of Acts. The preaching of Peter, Stephen, Paul, and the rest of the Apostles is fueled by the mighty prayer which brought the outpouring of the Holy Spirit at Pentecost. In revival preaching the preacher clearly comprehends his God-given authority and he proclaims Christ crucified to his hearers, giving the sense that God is the judge and jury, that all must stand before His awesome judgment seat and give account of their lives. It preaches for a verdict, calling people to act upon the word just preached. The revival preacher combines law and gospel, using the former to bring conviction of sin, and the latter to bring healing, redemption, and holiness. David Brainerd reports that the revival preaching at Crossweeksung evoked weeping and deep concern, not so much from the terrors of the Law but from the sweetness and goodness of God in salvation through Christ.[25]

There is a dearth of mighty preaching in the western church at this present time. We have the power, the unction of the Spirit available to us, and we seldom know the untold wealth this provides to the church and preacher. What is it? Is this a biblical concept? What results from it? How does a preacher get it? *First, we may define unction in preaching as a supernatural empowering and enabling by the Holy Spirit to do the Father's work for the glory of the Son.* Let's break this down a bit. Unction is supernatural. This has nothing to do with one's educational level, how gifted a communicator or orator he may be, how much experience he has, or how charismatic and engaging his personality is. It is supernatural. It is a work of the Holy Spirit. In fact, it is the Spirit Himself filling and dominating a man. To go further, unction is an empowering and enabling. By empowering I have in mind what we read in Luke 24:44-49 when, after the disciples had been with Jesus for three years and seen His remarkable ministry, after His resurrection, He told them to preach repentance for forgiveness of sins in His name to all the nations. However, they were to remain in the city until they had been clothed with power from on high. They dare not go forth in ministry without the Spirit's power and presence. Repeatedly we find the Greek words *exousia* (authority) and *dunamis* (power) used in reference to Jesus and His apostles and their earthly ministries. As only one example, consider Acts 1:8, "You shall receive power when the Holy Spirit comes upon you, and you shall be My witnesses both in Jerusalem, Judea, Samaria, and to the uttermost parts of the earth." Unction is the power of the Holy Spirit controlling, dominating, convicting, converting, and sanctifying. Unction is the enabling work of the

---

[25] *The Life of David Brainerd*, page 215ff.

Spirit. It gives the preacher insight into Scripture, the ability to gather the truth together in a clear, concise manner. It gives him the ability to drive home Biblical truth to his hearers so that they receive it, not merely as the word of men, but for what it really is, the Word of God, which also performs its work in those who believe (1 Thessalonians 2:13). When a preacher proclaims gospel truth in the power of the Holy Spirit his words, in effect, become the word of God to those with ears to ear.

In Romans 10:13ff Paul says, "Whoever will call upon the name of the Lord will be saved? And how then shall they call upon Him in whom they have not believed? And how shall they believe in Him whom they have not heard? And how shall they hear without a preacher? And how shall they preach unless they are sent. Just as it is written, 'How beautiful are the feet of those who bring glad tidings of good things!' However they did not all heed the glad tidings; for Isaiah says, 'Lord, who has received our message?' So faith comes by hearing and hearing by the word of Christ." Paul is thus saying that as the Holy Spirit works through the preacher, as the Spirit applies the truth to the hearers, then these become the very words of God to him. It is the Holy Spirit, the third person of the Trinity, who makes this possible. A preacher preaching with unction is preaching the words of God to his hearers.

And the unction is a specific work of God the Father. We find the anointing or unction of the Spirit in the Old Testament symbolically administered with oil. Oil was placed upon the heads of the prophets (1 Kings 19:16), priests (Exodus 28:41), and kings (1 Samuel 10:1). We know the Holy Spirit came upon people differently in the Old Testament times than from after Pentecost. He came upon people for specific purposes. Thus we find Bezalel being filled with the Spirit in wisdom, in understanding, in knowledge, and in all kinds of craftsmanship so that he may have the skill necessary to build the instruments of the tabernacle (Exodus 31:2-4). This anointing also carried with it the idea of consecration (Exodus 30:30, Leviticus 8:12). These men were set apart by God for their specific works on behalf of Yahweh, the King of glory. This "coming or going" of the Spirit explains why David, after his sin with Bathsheba said, "Do not cast me away from Thy presence, and do not take Thy Holy Spirit away from me," (Psalm 51:11).

This Holy Spirit anointing is a means of power, vitality, and fruitfulness in the preacher's life and ministry. No doubt there are times in every preacher's life when he is overwhelmed with fatigue, discouragement, and a sense of powerlessness. The anointing of the Spirit can be a source of strength and power spiritually, physically, and emotionally. We read in 1 Kings 18 of Obadiah, a servant of wicked King Ahab, who nonetheless, was a godly man who preserved the lives of one hundred young prophets of God from a purging by wicked Queen Jezebel. While on a search for water, due to the drought God brought through Elijah's prayers, Obadiah ran into Elijah. Elijah told him to have Ahab meet him at Mount Carmel for a showdown with the 450 prophets of Baal and the 400 prophets of Asherah. As we know, the prophets of Baal called all day for their god to consume the sacrifice but nothing happened. Elijah prayed down fire from heaven which utterly burned up the offering. The Holy Spirit gave Elijah the spiritual power he needed to fight the battle against Baal and Asherah. Later, as clouds form in the distance, Ahab and Elijah both watch as the clouds opened, pouring rain on the parched land. Ahab rode in his chariot from Mount Carmel to Jezreel in the fruitful plain between Jerusalem and the Sea of Galilee, while Elijah outran Ahab and his chariot, a distance of some thirty miles, farther than a marathon! How did Elijah have that strength? The Spirit empowered him! And later in 1 Kings 19, after hearing that Jezebel is still keen on having Elijah killed, he flees first to Beersheba and eventually to the Sinai Peninsula, a distance of well over two hundred miles. Elijah wanted to die, but the Spirit ministered to him, not by the earthquake, wind, or fire; but by a gentle voice (1 Kings 19:11-14). God strengthened Elijah emotionally.

If you are a pastor, then you know the plague of discouragement, the temptation to quit and find another line of work. This discouragement comes in many forms. You know you battle indwelling sin daily and sometimes your sin seems to get the best of you. You are alarmed and fearful of the thoughts that enter your mind, of the words which privately come out of your mouth. And then there is the discouragement of trouble in your marriage. You know what it is to live with disappointment with your wife. Perhaps you have grown cold in your devotion to her, secretly longing for another woman. And then your children can be a means of discouragement, even when they are relatively young. Perhaps you have seen sinful patterns in them that look very similar to what you see in yourself, and you know they learned these from you! And what pastor has not heard discouraging words from church officers? Even if the words are meant as "constructive criticism" they, nonetheless, sting all the same. And sooner or later most every pastor experiences church division, people leaving in droves, blaming you for their departure. "You cannot preach . . . you are not feeding me with your sermons . . . I get more out of the preacher at the church down the street . . . my children need a better youth ministry . . ."

My dear friends, we must have the anointing of the Holy Spirit upon our ministries, not merely in our preaching, but in everything—our teaching, counseling, leading, administrating, discipling, and our evangelizing. We need supernatural enabling in every spiritual dimension of ministry. The work of regeneration and sanctification is simply impossible. You are no match for the secularization of our culture, the immense problems of people in your community. And we need supernatural power in the physical dimension of our lives. Many times, especially after arriving in another country, eight or nine time zones away, I have been called upon to preach and was totally exhausted; but I have also seen God supernaturally empower me physically to deliver a message I know was not given in my own strength. We need the Spirit's anointing physically. Whitefield knew this first hand. He often would enter a new town on horseback, ravaged with fever, having already preached two or three times that same day, physically and emotionally exhausted. But as he began to preach the Spirit came upon him and he caught fire, and was used mightily of God. And we need His anointing emotionally. Ministry is not for the faint of heart and discouragement can threaten to undo you, but the Spirit can meet you powerfully and lift you up with great joy, boldness, and resolve to stay on task.

How do you receive the anointing of the Holy Spirit? Two things are clear. First, you must have faith. "Without faith it is impossible to please God," (Hebrews 11:6). "Ask and you shall receive. Seek and you shall find. Knock and the door shall be opened to you," (Matthew 7:7). "If you, being evil, know how to give good gifts to your children, how much will the Father give the Holy Spirit to those who ask Him," (Luke 11:13). "Until now you have asked for nothing in My name. Ask and you shall receive that your joy may be made full," (John 16:24). Simply believe what God says. But second, you must earnestly seek Christ. David says, "O God, Thou art my God. I shall seek Thee earnestly. My soul thirsts for Thee. My flesh yearns for Thee, in a dry and weary land where there is no water. Thus I have seen Thee in the sanctuary, to see Thy power and Thy glory," (Psalm 63:1-2). There is no substitute for earnestly seeking God like a thirsty man does water. Go into the sanctuary of God daily, expectantly, looking for and receiving a word from the living God!

Third, mighty prayer and mighty preaching always give way to mighty conversions. Every major revival witnesses millions of conversions in a one to two hundred year period. This happened in the Roman Empire in the first two hundred years of the New Testament church. It happened in Europe in the sixteenth century under Luther, Calvin, Zwingli, et al. It happened in the seventeenth century Puritan awakening in England and the American Colonies. It happened in America, England, Scotland, and Wales in the eighteenth century Great Awakening. It happened throughout the ever expanding American continent in the nineteenth century, as well as in England and Northern Ireland. It continues to happen in East Africa through the East African revival which began in the early 1950's. It is happening today in China, India, South America, and in many Muslim nations like Iran, Iraq, and Algeria.

On the day of Pentecost, three thousand were saved. A few days later we read of the church numbering five thousand men. Soon after we hear of people being added daily to the church. In a revival culture there are conversions every week. Today in the western church, we think we are blessed when we see one or two, three or four conversions per year. How many people are being saved through your church ministry? Probably very few. My brethren, these things ought not to be. At the very least, we should be deeply grieved over the lack of conversions. This fact ought to promote an intolerable burden to fast and pray, to ask, "Am I the blockage to the salvation of souls? Am I the problem?"

Fourth, mighty prayer, mighty preaching, and mighty conversions always give way to mighty assemblies. In Acts 4:31 we are told that the church gathered together and prayed and was filled with the Holy Spirit. Consequently the place where they were gathered was shaken and they spoke the word of God with boldness. Peter told the Sanhedrin when they forbid him to speak any longer in the name of Christ that he could not stop speaking what he had seen and heard, (Acts 4:20). A mighty assembly is the gathering of God's covenant people on the Lord's Day when a heart felt sense of the Spirit's presence falls upon the congregation like the Shekinah of Old Testament times (Exodus 40:38). A mighty assembly always results in Psalm 2 worship, "Worship the Lord with reverence, and rejoice with trembling. Do homage to the Son lest He become angry and you perish in the way," (Psalm 2:11). A sense of awe overcomes the people of God. A mighty assembly occurs when the people of God meet regularly, not only on the Lord's Day, but throughout the week in small groups, encouraging one another, praying for one another, holding one another to gospel holiness.

A number of years ago my wife and I were privileged to take tea with Lord and Lady Catherwood at Cambridge, England. Lady Catherwood is the daughter of the great Welsh preacher Martyn Lloyd-Jones. Since I had read all I could about her esteemed father, I was peppering Lady Catherwood with question after question about his life and ministry. At one point I asked her to describe what she saw in her father's ministry at Aberavon, Wales, when so many were being converted in the 1930's. Though she was only a child at the time, she said that it was unforgettable. "We could feel the presence of the Holy Spirit in those services." Iain Murray, in his biography of Lloyd-Jones[26] tells of a witch engaged in witchcraft who came to an evening service at the time. She came out of curiosity but continued to attend each Sunday night for a year. She finally was converted and joined the church. When asked by Lloyd-Jones her first impression of the church, she, being very much in tune with the spirit world, said, "I immediately sensed a clean spirit in this place." That's what I mean by a mighty assembly.

---

[26] *David Martyn Lloyd-Jones: The First Forty Years.*

Brainerd, in reporting on the mighty movement of God among the Indians at Creekweeksung, writes, "Divine truth fell with weight and power upon the audience, and seemed to reach the hearts of many. . . the word seemed to be accompanied by divine influence, and made powerful impressions upon the assembly in general."[27] Throughout church history mighty assemblies have resulted in the unbeliever's curiosity being aroused, leading him to visit public assemblies, often ending in his conversion as he sees the mighty works of God in the conversion of many.[28]

Can your church services, prayer meetings, and small group Bible studies be described as mighty assemblies?

And fifth, mighty assemblies lead to mighty holiness. Paul commends the Thessalonians for their faith, stating how they had turned from idols to serve the true and living God, (1 Thessalonians 1:9); and he also commends the Macedonians, saying that they had given out of their poverty to the Jewish believers in Jerusalem, (2 Corinthians 8:2). Neither a church nor its community is experiencing true revival if the level of morality and holiness is not raised. Simply put—Christians are to be different from the world, and holiness is that difference. In a revival culture, people put away their sin in dramatic fashion. If in most church settings, a few people, here and there, who have marital problems, experience some measure of healing through months and months of counseling; if a few people addicted to internet pornography gain a measure of freedom from this enslavement; if one or two per year gain a gradual control over the chronic anger problems, then we consider these victories of holiness. And I am not disparaging these days of small things. However in a revival culture many people are almost immediately delivered from their various forms of sinful bondage. They live lives of freedom and joy. The transforming and sanctifying power of the gospel is evident to all within the church. Those coming out of such sinful patterns have little desire to go back to their previous ways.

Does this mark your church? Are you seeing this level of growth in biblical holiness among your church members?

Sixth, mighty holiness leads to mighty personal evangelism. In Acts 8:1ff we read that the people were dispersed from Jerusalem due to persecution, that they continued going about evangelizing (the actual Greek word in Acts 8:4 is *evangelize*). In Romans 1:8 Paul commends the Romans, telling them that their faith is being proclaimed throughout the whole world, giving one the impression that Roman believers were already taking the gospel to the nations. In 1 Thessalonians 1:8 Paul commends these Macedonian believers in similar fashion, saying that the word of the Lord has sounded forth from them, not only in Macedonia, their region; but also in Achaia, much further south. In fact their faith in every place has gone forth. He has no reason to preach the gospel there for they have been doing it themselves. And when Peter and John are arrested by the Sanhedrin, put in jail over night, released, and commanded not to preach any further, they say, "We cannot stop speaking about what we have seen and heard," (Acts 4:20). Evangelism is not left to

---

[27] *The Life of David Brainerd,* pages 198-199.

[28] The Welsh revival beginning in 1735 is a good case in point. On more than one occasion Howell Harris' life was threatened by evil doers, who in the end attended the meetings and were soundly converted. See *The Calvinistic Methodist Fathers of Wales.*

pastors and missionaries when revival is in the air. The whole church engages in her God-given responsibility—to make disciples of all the nations. Brainerd had little response among the Indians at the forks of the Delaware River, but after those at Crossweeksung were converted, he took them to the Delaware River and they bore witness to God's mighty work among their own people, moving the formerly hard hearted and scoffing Indians to listen and embrace Christ.[29] Similarly Don Richardson, John Dekker, and many other missionaries traveled with their families to Papua New Guinea in the early 1960's to evangelize the primitive, cannibalistic tribal peoples of that place. Those converted immediately had a burden to take the good news of reconciliation and deliverance to their mortal enemies in nearby villages, resulting in wholesale conversions of entire tribes.[30] The church is the base of operations for evangelistic outreach. She is to engage in it. Anything less is an incomplete picture of gospel holiness. Personal evangelism is a mark of one's personal holiness.

Are you regularly speaking to others about what you have seen and heard? Are those in your church, all the believers there, speaking about the mighty deeds of salvation? With a few exceptions, we are ineffectual in reaching our modern, western culture. We have never had more training, more books, more seminars, more teaching on personal evangelism and every other conceivable ministry in the church, but we continue to lose ground. So few open their mouths to speak of Jesus. Are you possessed by a guilty silence concerning gospel proclamation?

Seventh, mighty personal evangelism leads to mighty generosity and compassion. Believers in Macedonia and Achaia, in the great ordeal of their affliction were giving out of their poverty to those in Jerusalem. According to their ability and beyond their ability they were giving to the needs of their Jewish brethren (2 Corinthians 8:1-3). And in Philippians Paul commends the Macedonians, reminding them that they were the only church who contributed to his needs after he had left Macedonia, and that more than once they gave to him while he was in Thessalonica (Philippians 4:15-16). Barnabas gave his property to the Lord's work (Acts 4:36-37), and the people held all things in common, meeting the practical needs of all the brethren in Jerusalem (Acts 4:32-34). For the Macedonians to give out of their poverty is like a village of Teso Christians in Uganda giving from their meager resources to ease the pain of the Haitians after the January, 2010 earthquake.

In a revival culture mighty generosity always manifests itself in plenty of resources to do the work of the gospel. Missionaries don't have to wait for three years or more, itinerating all over the country, trying to scrape together the money to cover their salaries and budgets. Churches have enough money to pay needed staff and to fund mercy ministries in their inner cities.

Eighth, mighty generosity always leads, sooner or later, to mighty societal impact. At the beginning of his third missionary journey, Paul the apostle, comes to Ephesus and begins teaching his disciples in the school of Tyrannus (Acts 19:8ff). He does so for three years and God does mighty things there. Not only are there as many as ten churches planted

---

[29] *The Life of David Brainerd*, pages 219ff.

[30] See *Peace Child* by Don Richardson and *Torches of Joy: A Stone Age Tribe's Encounter With the Gospel,* by John Dekker

directly and indirectly through his ministry[31], but gospel power is driving out demonic possession as well. So many witchdoctors were being converted that they brought their very expensive books of canticles used in their demonology, along with their fetishes, and burned them before the Lord, proclaiming to everyone that they were done with their former lives. Even exorcists, watching the Apostle Paul in action, were seeking to mimic him, much, however, to their own embarrassment and personal harm (Acts 19:13-16). And do we not also see there in Ephesus that a riot breaks out at the hands of the silversmiths who are angry because the populace no longer is buying their silver trinkets related to the worship of Diana. That's because these Ephesians have turned from their idols to serve the living God!

When homosexual King Mwanga of Uganda burned alive two dozen young boys, who had recently come to faith in Christ, because they refused to have sexual relations with him, the martyrdom brought the outpouring of the Holy Spirit upon Uganda, bringing the salvation of thousands, bringing a reign of peace in the country for many years.[32]

Regardless of what television preachers and others may be saying about mighty movements of God in and through their ministries, one of the infallible and biblical proofs of true revival is societal impact. If today in the United States, we saw a Great Awakening like that in New England in the eighteenth century when ten percent of the population was converted, then most of our problems with pornography, inner city crime and poverty, children born outside of marriage, murder, drug dealing, white collar crime, political corruption, abortion, same sex marriage, and many more would quickly dissipate. What we need are many true conversions which would bring a mighty transformation of our culture. Some have criticized men like R.J. Rushdooney and Greg Bahnsen for being theonomists[33], but they repeatedly say that we can never force people to obey God's law. This only comes when there are millions of conversions by the regenerating work of the Holy Spirit. When this happens, people will gladly submit to God's law.

So, surely you will agree with me that we know next to nothing of societal impact in our ministries in the western world. Should we not admit our impotence, asking God to provoke within us an intolerable burden, an intense grief over the status quo in our own lives, in the church, and in the world?

Ninth, mighty societal impact results in mighty leadership. God brings forth pastors, teachers, evangelists, elders, and deacons when revival comes to a church and community. Leaders are necessary to propel a congregation out into the world to evangelize, speak the truth in love, and to serve the needy both within and without the

---

[31] We know of the seven churches of Asia Minor from Revelation 2-3—Ephesus, Smyrna, Pergamum, Thyatira, Sardis, Philadelphia, and Laodicea, but also churches are mentioned in nearby Colossae and Miletus. Finally there was a church in the home of Nympha, Colossians 4:15-16.

[32] For a fuller and very inspiring story see *St. Charles Lwanga and Companions, Martyrs of Uganda* <www.catholic.org/saints>

[33] The world *theonomy* comes from two Latin words *Theos*-God and *nomos*-law, and it refers to God's law as the standard by which any nation ought to live. The seminal theonomic work is Rushdoony's *Institutes of Biblical Law.*

congregation. Paul instructed Titus to appoint elders in every city (Titus 1:5), and Paul was constantly including men on his missionary tours, preparing them for leadership roles in the work of Christ's church (Acts 13:13, 15:36, 40, 18:1-3, 19:9, 20:1-6, 17, 1, 2 Timothy, Titus). In the days of the Great Awakening, especially in Wales and England, God worked mightily through Welsh preachers like Daniel Rowland and Howell Harris and the English Methodist, John Wesley, to raise up laymen who shepherded and discipled those converted through the preaching ministries of these three men. In India today, we are seeing something similar through ministries like *Operation Mobilization* with its indigenous leadership. Among the Dalit people, God is raising up leaders in this growing church. In his still vitally important book[34] Roland Allen contrasts the Apostolic methodology found in Acts and the Pastoral epistles with how we groom leaders today. Then, elders were appointed very quickly and they were given authority to lead the church. We, however, take a man out of his natural environment (say an inner city young black man, put a tie on him, make him go to seminary and get a few degrees, by that time his friends have died and he no longer can relate to them anyway[35]), requiring an inordinate and unnecessary level of education and training. Very often he has lost his zeal and efficacy after we have finished with him. We are not trusting the Spirit to raise up and anoint leaders. I am not saying that formal theological training is unnecessary for everyone. By all means we need theologians to keep us on track, to warn us of heresy; but do we need trained theologians working in the hood or the barrio?

If your church is not regularly seeing young men go into full time ministry, then surely your church is lacking. In a revival culture this is happening on a large scale.

And tenth, mighty leadership brings mighty opposition. There are at least four sources of this opposition to the work of the gospel when revival is happening. First, the main opponent to revival is ourselves. We do not experience revival personally because we do not seek God for it. James says, "Draw near to God, and He will draw near to you (James 4:__). We suffer the "affliction of affluence" in the west. We have it so easy. We have all the modern day comforts, and these invariably mitigate zeal for Christ's kingdom expansion.

The devil is a roaring lion, seeking to devour whomever he may, (1 Peter 5:8). When the gospel begins to attack the societal and cultural depravity prevalent in any culture, then the forces of evil do not take it sitting down. They rise up and bring an onslaught of persecution, lies, and division upon the church. Revival heightens this spiritual conflict. The devil is in the details of ministry. How many times have we all seen a ministry threatened because someone did not follow through with the details! The opposition, however, does not merely come from the devil. The world, when the church "gets off the reservation" and begins to address societal ills from God's word, gets highly indignant and feels threatened. Have you noticed lately how we are told by government leaders that we ought to fight for the "freedom of worship." This is a change from the earlier and more conventional idea of "freedom of religion." The latter carries with it the notion that we are free to believe what we want, in the public and well as private sectors of our society. Now, however, the terminology has been cleverly changed. Now we are free to worship (on whatever our holy day may be), but the unspoken expectation is that we

---

[34] *The Spontaneous Expansion of the Church*, published in 1925.

[35] For a powerful word on this lamentable situation I refer you to the Christian rapper Lecrae and his song "Beautiful Feet."

restrict our religion to that holy day. Our worship is not to impact normal life, the other six days of the week. So in a revival culture the hostility of the world's system is provoked and rains down on believers in persecution and disenfranchisement. But we can go further and say this opposition is also on the inside of each of us. Perhaps the greatest opponent to a revival culture is the believer himself. Let's face it. We simply want our comfort. We don't want to be bothered. We like our own fleshly, secret lives. We love to come home at night, sit in front of the television, and do nothing. It takes effort, even heartache, to be involved in the lives of other people. It takes effort to seek God earnestly in fasting, grieving over personal sin, and earnest prayer. We risk ridicule when we venture forth with the gospel to our neighbors, family members, and work associates. We fear the sneer of the peer! But finally, and perhaps most surprisingly, we face opposition from the status quo religious establishment. It has always been this way. Read in the Old Testament how the prophets were regularly maligned, rejected, persecuted, and killed by the religious people of Israel and Judah. The religious were the ones who maligned, persecuted, and eventually killed the Lord Jesus. The tax-gatherers and sinners heard Him gladly. And the apostles, except for John, were all martyred as well. Indeed Jude vividly describes them as hidden reefs in our love feasts, calling them clouds without water, carried along by winds, autumn trees without fruit, doubly dead, uprooted, wild waves of he sea, casting up their own shame like foam, wandering stars, for whom the black darkness has been reserved forever . . . These are the ones who cause divisions, worldly minded, devoid of the Spirit (Jude 12-13, 19).

In a revival culture, we find the words of the Apostle Paul ringing true, "Those who desire to live godly in Christ Jesus will be persecuted," (2 Timothy 3:12). We also will know personally what Jesus means when He says, "Blessed are you when men revile you, persecute you, and say all kinds of evil things against you falsely on account of Me," (Matthew 5:10-11); "Woe to you if all men speak well of you," (Luke 6:26); "If the world hates you, you know that it hated Me before it hated you," (John 15:18). The very fact that we know next to nothing of opposition to the gospel is proof positive that we are not in a revival culture. Basically, our churches are irrelevant to our communities. We are a non-issue. This certainly was not the case with the apostles in Iconium, Lystra, Derbe, Philippi, Athens, Corinth, or Rome.

Oh, how we ought to long for revival in our nation and world! The Acts of the Apostles is normative. This is the benchmark for the church. Anything less is failure. Merely "being faithful" is not enough. These ten marks ought to be readily apparent, growing in intensity in our ministries. If they are not, then we are woefully inadequate. May God cause us to weep over our impotence, driving us to repentance and the pursuit of Biblical holiness! The church in the western world is languishing in unbelief, carnality, and worldliness. We have become milquetoast. May God stir us up to spend and be spent for the sake of the gospel, not only to save our western world, but more importantly, to show the world the glory of our great Christ, the Savior of sinners, the Lord of all the nations!

Part III: MAKING YOUR CHURCH A HOUSE OF PRAYER
FOR THE NATIONS

Chapter 6
The Godward Direction of Prayer

A cursory reading of John 2:13-22 where Jesus cleanses the temple may cause some to conclude that His action was spontaneous, that as He came into the temple, He saw for the first time how the money-changers were abusing the proper use of the temple. This cannot be true, however, because as a Jewish man Jesus would have made three trips each year to Jerusalem for the various religious observances. In fact in Luke 2 we are told that after such a visit, when He was twelve years old, Jesus remained behind and conversed with the religious leaders and they were amazed at his acumen. So Jesus had seen these abuses for at least thirty years of His life. Don Richardson, in his book, Eternity in Their Hearts[36], has noted that the court of the Gentiles, where the money-changers operated, was for the express purpose of the Jews praying for the ethne, the Gentile world, that they too would be grafted into the covenant between Yahweh and Israel. Instead these people were using it to change foreign money into the local currency to facilitate the purchase of animals needed in making sacrifices to Yahweh. So, as John tells us (John 2:15), Jesus made a whip and entered the temple, wielding His whip, driving the money-changers and animals from the temple. One can only imagine the sound of tables being overturned, gold and silver coins rolling on the floor, animals squealing, people running from the One who has eyes as a flame of fire. His disciples, in seeing this display of Jesus' holiness and zeal, remembered the Psalmist who said, "Zeal for Your house will consume Me," (Psalm 69:9). Jesus Himself said, in quoting Jeremiah 7:11 and Isaiah 56:7, "My house shall be called a house of prayer, but you are making it a robber's den," (Matthew 21;13). Mark has it, "My house shall be called a house of prayer for all the nations, but you have made it a robber's den," (Mark 11:17).

So the church of the Lord Jesus Christ, the blood bought people of the King of Kings and Lord of Lords, is to be a house of prayer for the nations, to fulfill the glorious words of John's vision, "Worthy art Thou, to take the book and to break its seals, for Thou wast slain and didst purchase for God with Thy blood, men from every tongue, tribe, people, and nation; and Thou hast made them to be a kingdom and priests to our God, and they will dwell upon the earth" (Revelation 5:9-10). Instead, however, the church has too often been a country club, an entertainment center, a place where people merely care for themselves, having forgotten their mission, to make disciples of all the nations (Matthew 28:18-20).

So the question before us now is this—how can your church become a house of prayer for the nations? First, we must briefly visit once again the foundation for this house of prayer. We have looked at this in detail earlier, but I bring it to your attention again. The house of prayer must be established on the twin pillars of the intolerable burden and contrition which leads to sincere, heartfelt repentance. You may remember that I defined the intolerable burden as an intense grief over the status quo in our personal lives, in the church, and in the world. Until we gain this, nothing else we do will matter. All the planning, programs, personalities, budgets, buildings, and gifts will not do. There must be a a major paradigm shift in today's church if we are to see God pour out His Spirit in true revival. Business as usual will not work. So, how do we gain this intolerable burden?

---

[36] *Eternity in their Hearts*

First, ask the Holy Spirit to show you the depth of your own personal sin. Think back to what you were like before God wrought a miracle of regenerating grace in your life, that which caused you to see your sin, to repent, and to run to Jesus for refuge. And think also of how, even as a believer, your thoughts are often wicked and perverse. Remind yourself that even now, you are capable of profound evil. You are capable of anything. Ask Him to show you the recurring sins in your mind, and flesh, the fact that you, at times, inwardly delight in them. And examine yourself, consider your values. Are you filled with pride, unwilling to receive rebuke from your spouse, from a close friend, from your pastor or elder? Have you left your first love? Have you lost your hunger for God's word? Do you find that you are seldom convicted of sin when reading the Bible or hearing a soul searching sermon? Do you seldom speak to others about their souls? Is your prayer time sketchy, passionless? Are you lukewarm, seldom concerned about the progress of the gospel in your community, in Muslim nations of the world? Are you robbing God, not giving Him His tithe, one-tenth of your income to His work? Surely, as you consider your heart, your values, your speech, and your actions you can see that you are not where you ought to be.

And then consider the church. First of all, your own church. Are the ten marks of the revival culture there? Is there mighty praying, mighty preaching, mighty conversions, mighty assemblies, mighty holiness, mighty generosity, mighty personal evangelism, mighty societal impact, mighty leadership, and mighty opposition? If not, and seldom are these marks seen today in the western church, then ask God to burden you deeply with the state of your own church. And then consider the church as a whole in your community, nation, and world. Will you not agree that the church is woefully weak, impotent, increasingly irrelevant in our culture? We tend to be devoid of heartfelt prayer. We are worldly, materialistic, addicted to the comforts of modernity. We have the health and wealth gospel, on the one hand; and on the other a formal, trivial, flippant, therapeutic, man-centered gospel that says to people, "It's all about me." Ask God to burden you with the state of the church in our world.

And then consider the world itself. The western world, going back to at least the Enlightenment, has rejected God, making man the measure of all things. Consequently, man has gone into the void[37]. Life increasingly has no meaning to him. There are no laws because there is no God, and because there is no God, there is no sin or judgment. Thus man is free to do as he pleases. Indeed, he lives antithetically to the God of the Bible. Whenever we reject God we choose death (Proverbs 8:36). This explains why we abort babies, have senseless drive by shootings, and mass murders on elementary school, high school, and college campuses. This explains the genocide that has so marked our world in the last one hundred years. Then, of course, there is the awful reality of hell for all who reject the only way of salvation (John 14:6, Acts 4:12). Tribulation and distress is upon every man who is contentious, who disobeys the truth, who obeys unrighteousness (Romans 2:8-9). God promises to deal out retribution for all who do not know Him, to all who do not obey the gospel of the Lord Jesus Christ (2 Thessalonians 1:8-9). Jesus makes clear that hell is a real place of conscious, endless torment (Mark 9:43-48, Luke 16:19-31). As bad as hell is, that is not the end for the damned. Their lot is far worse, for they will be cast into the lake of fire at the time of Jesus' second advent (Revelation 20:11-15). It will come to all whose names are not written in the Lamb's book of life (Revelation 21:8, 27). As you contemplate the awful reality of eternal perdition, does this

----

[37] *To Be As God: A Study of Modern Thought from the Marquis de Sade*, R. J. Rushdoony, page 131.

not move you to earnestness in prayer? If not then surely you need to search your heart, asking if you truly believe the Bible. Our God is a consuming fire (Hebrews 12:29). It is a terrifying thing to fall into the hands of the living God (Hebrews 10:31).

But not only do we need an intolerable burden, we must also grieve over our sin with sincere contrition, leading to true, evangelical repentance, that which brings change in our lives. John the Baptist told those coming for baptism that they were to bring forth fruit in keeping with repentance (Matthew 3:8). Coming without repentance showed that they were still a brood of vipers capable of great destruction. They were still under the wrath of God without repentance. The three foundational sins—pride, unbelief, and rebellion— must be cleared from the highway of holiness. These must be removed if God is to come upon us by a visitation of His Holy Spirit. Consider again the latent pride in your flesh and mind. Are you unwilling to accept rebuke? Do you think you are better than others of a different race, ethnicity, socio-economic background, educational or professional level? Do you smirk at other believers with a less developed theological system than yours. Do you pay lip service to prayer, but actually trust your own ability, experience, and expertise to accomplish your ministry, to lead your family, to develop your business?

Is your life characterized by unbelief? Do you doubt the sufficiency of God's word? Do you question its authority? Do you argue privately about what it says concerning those of other religions, those who embrace same sex marriage? Do you say you trust the Father but find your life consistently plagued with doubt, anxiety, and worry? Do you find it difficult or impossible to forgive others who have wronged you, ripped you off at some point in your business or personal life? Do you doubt the efficacy of Christ's death truly to take away your sin, to remove your guilt and shame, to give you the power to walk in gospel holiness? Do you doubt the words of Peter who says that we have all we need pertaining to life and godliness (2 Peter 1:3)? Do you look first to medication to help you through your down times? And do you doubt the efficacy and power of the Holy Spirit to convert family members who are far away from the Lord? Have you lost hope for our country, concerning our present, godless, and perverse way of life?

And is your life characterized by downright, abject rebellion against God? You know what He expects of you concerning personal purity, but do you continue to visit internet porn sites? You know God commands you to tithe, and you continue to give Him a pittance of your income. You know you are to love your wife sacrificially, to live with her in an understanding way, to put her needs before your own, to lead her spiritually; but you refuse to do any of these. You know you are to submit to your husband, to win him without a word, but you continue to nag him, you continue to go your own way, refusing to honor him as your husband. You know you are to speak the truth at all times, but you continue to deceive, tell half-truths, and put yourself in a better light than you deserve. I could go on and on, but you get the point, don't you? Until we repent, until we feel our sin deeply, leading to grieving over our sin, what theologians call contrition, then we will not see revival. All that follows in making our churches houses of prayer for the nations will not work without a firm foundation. The foundation is essential. You must have an intolerable burden, and you must feel deeply your sin, leading to true repentance.

Having stated emphatically the foundation on which the house of prayer for the nations must be built, I now move to the first four living stones that make up the house of prayer for the nations. I am speaking here of revival prayer. There is a God-ward element to these four living stones. Of course all prayer is directed to God, but I have in mind here a preoccupation with the God whom we approach in revival prayer. I also suggest there is an order in which these living stones are used to build the house of prayer for the nations. The first living stone is this—we must pray with the heart of Jesus. Now I mean two things with this statement. First, to pray with the heart of Jesus means you must have His heart, if you are to pray. That is, you must be born again. Jesus told Nicodemus that no one can see the kingdom of God unless he is born again (John 3:3). Ezekiel, the Old Testament prophet, said the same thing in a different way. He said, "Moreover, I will give you a new heart, and put My Spirit within you. I will take out the heart of stone from your flesh, and give you a heart of flesh," (Ezekiel 36:26). God only hears the prayers of His people (Isaiah 59:1-2, John 9:31). A non-Christian, no matter how sincere he is, no matter if he is a Presbyterian, Baptist, Roman Catholic, Muslim, Mormon, Hindu, or animist will not find his prayers answered by God. He is not a child of God. In fact, according to Jesus, he is a child of the devil (John 8:44).

But secondly, when I speak of having the heart of Jesus I also mean you must pray with the heart of Jesus. That is, you must pray for those things on His heart, those things He values most. We can look many places in Scripture for this information, but I suggest a cursory look at the Lord's Prayer (Matthew 6:9-13). There we find six petitions Jesus teaches us to pray to His heavenly Father.[38] If you frame your prayers in these six petitions, then you can be sure you are praying with the heart of Jesus. You will be praying for those things on His heart. Remember, James tells us that we have not, because we ask not, and we ask and do not receive, because we ask with wrong motives to spend it on our pleasures (James 4:2-3).

Okay, so what do these six petitions mean? First, Jesus teaches us to pray, "Hallowed by Thy name." In other words, you should pray like this, "My gracious, loving, all powerful heavenly Father, the One who loves me with an everlasting love, I ask that You work in me a fervent, zealous, and persistent desire to glorify You in all I do." To glorify God, simply put, is to make God look good in all you think, do, and say. We are to magnify his grace, mercy, love, patience, and kindness to all people. We are to conduct ourselves in a way that honors Him, that projects to a watching world His holiness, truth, justice, and mercy.

And second, Jesus prays, "Thy kingdom come." Jesus' desire is for the nations (Psalm 67, 47). He longs to see those from every tongue, tribe, people, and nation around His throne, a throng which no one can number, giving praise to Him (Revelation 7:9-12). So we should pray with a keen interest for the progress of the gospel around the world. We should learn to read the news with "Great Commission eyes." That is, when considering the geo-political situation in the Middle East, for example, don't focus so much on what the news reporters are telling us about the various factions vying for control. Instead ask, "God what are You doing in the midst of all this? Would You work through the uncertainty, poverty, death, and destruction to drive people to the Lord Jesus for refuge?" So, when you pray with a kingdom focus, then God is honored and you are very well on your way to see God answer your prayers in a powerful fashion.

And third, Jesus prays, "Thy will be done, on earth as it is in heaven." By this Jesus means that are to trust Him, to submit to our loving Father in every circumstance without grumbling or complaining. Because He is our Father who loves us, and knows what is

---

[38] For a wonderful and full exposition of these six petitions, I suggest you study the *Larger Catechism of the Westminster Confession of Faith,* Questions 190-195

best for us, we can trust Him, delighting in all that happens to us, regardless of the immediate hardship His "frowning providence" may bring our way. So, we should pray, "Father, please work in my life in such a way that regardless of what You bring my way, regardless of the good and the bad, that I will be able to trust You, to delight in You, knowing that You will work everything for good in my life in due time."

And fourth, Jesus prays, "Give us this day, our daily bread." We tend so flippantly to pray this petition without considering its meaning. How many of us can really pray this with sincerity? How many of us would really be content with only enough basic food for this very day? Of course many people in our world live in just this manner, but most of you reading this can never make that claim. But to pray this prayer is to acknowledge that due to our own fall into sin, we are unworthy of anything from God, that we have squandered His beneficence. Nonetheless this prayer also means that we are acknowledging our total dependence upon God for everything, even the basic necessities of life, that we gain nothing at all by our own devices. So you can pray, "Father, I realize that all I have is from You, that I deserve nothing but Your wrath on my life, but You have redeemed me by the precious blood of Your Son, and You say that no good thing will You withhold from those who walk uprightly (Psalm 84:11). So I ask that You meet the basic needs of my family and those around me, especially my brothers and sisters in Christ who suffer in poverty and hardship."

And fifth, Jesus prays, "Forgive us our debts, as we forgive our debtors." Here's what Jesus means by this petition, based also on what He says in Matthew 18:23-35, and what Paul says in Ephesians 4:32. If you are in Christ Jesus, then God has forgiven you a debt you could never repay. If you live perfectly from this time forward, if you do marvelous deeds of kindness for the next one thousand years, you can still never work off, or pay back the debt you owe God. He is absolutely perfect, and He demands that you be perfect, just like Him (Matthew 5:48), but you continually sinned against His kindness and grace to you. You have broken each of His Ten Commandments times without number. The certificate of debt, consisting of decrees against you, looms over your life at all times (Colossians 2:13-14). If God were to mark your iniquities, you could never stand. Let's say you committed only three sins per day. That's still one thousand per year. When you are sixty years old, then you have committed at least sixty thousand sins. Can God simply forget about your sin? You know He cannot because He is absolutely holy and just. He will not leave the guilty unpunished (Exodus 34:7). But He has forgiven you through the precious, redeeming, reconciling, propitiating, expiating blood of His Son (Isaiah 53:4-12, Romans 3:25, 1 John 4:10). Now, because God has forgiven you this great debt, you are to forgive others the lesser debt they owe you. That's what Jesus is driving at in Matthew 18:22ff when He tells Peter he is to forgive seventy times seven. Let's be clear, people have wronged you. No doubt you have been cheated, ripped off, and hurt by others. They owe you big time, but you have a choice. You can either harbor their sin against you, or you can release them of their obligation, of their debt. Think of it this way—let's say you loan a friend one thousand dollars and he promises to repay you within six months. So six months comes and goes, and he has not repaid you. You let it go for a few weeks, but you are pretty perturbed that your friend has not honored his contract with you. Finally you call him, asking when he will repay you. He says, "Please give me a another couple of weeks, and I will get the money to you." A few weeks goes by and still no repayment. So now it becomes clear to you that you are not going to get your money back. You have a choice to make. You can remain bitter and resentful, or you can forgive the debt. You can write it off. Now if you write off the debt, then you must not bring this up in your mind again. Let it go. Release your friend from the debt he owes you.

So, to pray this petition goes something like this, "Father, I now realize You have forgiven me an enormous debt that I could never repay in a million years, and I thank You for Your kindness and grace to me. Now, Father, You know that Harry wronged me by maligning me to others, and this has brought me great harm. But because You have forgiven me my great debt against You, I choose to forgive Harry of the wrong he has done me." Forgiveness, based on God's mercy to us is essential if we are to engage in revival prayer, if we are make our churches a house of prayer for the nations.

And finally, Jesus prays, "Lead us not into temptation, but deliver us from evil." James the apostle gives us insight into the meaning of this petition for he writes, "Let no one say when he is tempted, 'I am being tempted by God,' for God does not tempt anyone, and He Himself is not tempted; but each one is tempted when he is carried away and enticed by his own lusts, and when lust is conceived it gives birth to sin, and when sin is accomplished, it brings forth death," (James 1:13-14). So, while God does not bring temptation on us, He does ordain everything that happens in our lives, including trials (James 1:2-4) which fall, sometimes suddenly upon us, out of the blue, so to speak. God is there with the trial, but the devil is right behind Him in the same circumstance, waiting to tempt us. God means these trials for our growth in grace. The devil means these temptations to destroy us. So, pray this way, "Father, I do not trust myself, that is my flesh, for I know no good things dwells there. I know my own indwelling sin and inward lusts can easily be enticed by devilish temptations. Therefore, I ask that You not allow these temptations to come upon me, for I fear what I might do, and if I succumb to them, then I will bring great shame to Your name, something I cannot bear to consider. And, if in Your most wise providence, You do allow temptations to come my way, I beseech You to give me the grace to stand strong against them. And if You allow them to come, and if I fall in them, I then ask You for the grace of repentance and restoration, that You will use even my sinful failures to Your glory and my growth in grace."

So, first of all. We must learn to pray with the heart of Jesus. But second, we must also pray in the name of Jesus. Jesus says, "Truly, truly I say to you, if you ask the Father for anything in My name, He will give it to you. Until now you have asked for nothing in My name. Ask and you shall receive so that your joy may be made full," (John 16:23-24). He also says, "Whatever you ask in My name, that will I do, so that the Father may be glorified in the Son. If you ask Me anything in My name, I will do it," (John 14:13-14). So to pray in the name of Jesus is not some superstitious ritual. To pray in the name of Jesus has in mind at least two things. First, Jesus is the "broker", the go-between of the covenant of grace, the only mediator between God and man (1 Timothy 1:5, Hebrews 7:25). He alone makes access to the Father possible because He is the only pure and perfect High Priest. All the Old Testament high priests were mere men like us, prone to sinful folly and weakness. But second, the name of Jesus, more specifically, the Lord Jesus Christ, is a name of unparalleled glory, efficacy, and power. He is Lord—the sovereign, almighty king, whose robe is dipped in blood, who has a sharp two-edged sword coming out of His mouth, who has the seven stars in His right hand, the One who treads the winepress of the fierce wrath of God the Almighty. He is Jesus—the One who is mighty to save, who takes our sins from us as far as the east is from the west, who delivers us from the domain of darkness and transfers us into the kingdom of His Father, the One who cancels out the certificate of debt consisting in decrees or charges against us, having nailed them to the cross. And He is the Christ—the only One with the Spirit anointed three-fold office of prophet (the One who teaches us truth), priest (the One who makes access to the Father possible), and king (the ruler of the kings of the earth). It is to this Jesus that every knee will bow, and every tongue will confess that He is Lord to the glory of God the Father (Philippians 2:10-11).

And third, we must learn to pray the word of God. This is extremely important, and something many believers fail to consider or practice. We want and need revival prayer and this comes by praying the will of God, and the will of God is found in God's word. Jesus said, "If you abide in Me, and My words abide in you, ask whatever you wish, and it will be done for you," (John 15:7). John said, "This is the confidence which we have before Him, that, if we ask anything according to His will, He hears us. And if we know that He hears us in whatever we ask, we know that we have the requests which we have asked from Him," (1 John 5:14-15). It has been my observation that prayer power, prayer on which the Holy Spirit descends, is more extended in length. I am not saying that so-called conversational prayer (where people pray a sentence or two, and then someone else adds to the prayer or moves onto another request) is wrong. By no means. I am saying, however, that I have seldom, if ever, found this kind of prayer lifting people up into the presence of God. This experience seems to happen only when people pray for several minutes, allowing the Spirit to energize them and those praying with them. The problem, however, for most of us is that we have our own, little pet phrases we use in prayer, which may or may not be inspired by Scripture. You know what I mean, don't you —"God, please give us traveling mercies on the trip . . . Father, please lead, guide, and direct us . . . Father God, we just want to praise You . . . " Most of us run out of material really fast in this kind of prayer. However if we pray the word of God, and we can go for long, extended periods of time, thirty minutes to an hour, or even longer. I will assure you, from personal experience, having been with mighty prayer warriors, having heard them pray for these extended periods of time, that the Holy Spirit visits these prayer times with His sanctifying presence and power. These are, indeed, times of refreshment from the presence of the Lord.

So, how does one pray the word of God. Consider the many examples in Scripture of men and women praying the word of God (Nehemiah 1, Daniel 9, Matthew 6:9-13, Ephesians 1:18-19, Ephesians 3:14-19, Colossians 1:9-11, Philippians 1:9-11). The simplest way to pray the word of God is to take one of these prayers and make it your own. Or take any passage of Scripture and turn it into a prayer. I was in a revival prayer meeting one time, after teaching on this very subject, and a woman, who had never prayed publicly, took her Bible, opened it to Psalm 2 and proceeded to turn this into a wonderful prayer, one verse at a time. By the time she finished praying the Psalm, she had prayed simply but powerfully for twenty minutes or so. She was surprised and thrilled! Or take the main points of your pastor's sermon from the previous Sunday and turn them into a prayer. Just as you may take a passage and teach the main points to someone, so take the same passage and turn it into a prayer to God. You will find that you can pray much longer, much more Biblically, much more expectantly, and much more powerfully. I cannot underestimate the vital necessity of praying the word of God.

But fourth and finally, we must learn to pray in the Spirit. In Ephesians 6:18 Paul says, "With all prayer and petition, pray at all times in the Spirit." Now, what does he mean by this? It means to pray until you pray. Pray until the Spirit grabs your heart and you become lost in the glory of God's presence. The seventeenth century Puritans, the old line Pentecostals, and the Wesleyans all had a similar expression to explain what it meant to pray in the Spirit. They would speak of "praying through." I had an old Pentecostal friend in Connecticut whom I would regularly visit in a nursing home, and he would always ask me, after I had returned from leading a day of revival prayer, "Well, brother, did you pray through?" To pray in the Spirit means to be under the direct influence of the Spirit when you and the others with you are praying. Think of it this way—you no doubt have found yourself needing to give a word of comfort to someone in the midst of untold grief. You did not know what to say, but the Holy Spirit came upon you and gave you just the right words of comfort. Or perhaps you had an opportunity to share Jesus with someone and you were amazed at how your words helped explain the gospel to your friend. How did this happen? The Holy Spirit gave you unction, divine felicity of speech, a supernatural eloquence you do not normally have. In the same way, to pray in the Holy Spirit means the Spirit gives you the words to say. I have seen people who are slow, and very halting in their normal speech, get caught up in the Spirit and pray with unusual felicity and eloquence.

So, if we are to make our churches a house of prayer for the nations, if we are to engage in revival prayer, then we must pray with the heart of Jesus, we must pray in the name of Jesus, we must pray the word of God, and we must pray in the Holy Spirit. So, I challenge you to implement these four living stones in your own prayer life. You will see a great improvement if you do.

Part III: MAKING YOUR CHURCH A HOUSE OF PRAYER
FOR THE NATIONS

Chapter 7
Inwardly, Focusing on Your Growth

The prophet Daniel was around fourteen years old when, along with some 10,000 of his countrymen, he was sent away into exile to Babylon, or modern day Iraq. While in Babylon, we see (in Daniel 9) that he was reading the prophet Jeremiah and discovered that Yahweh had prophesied a return from the exile after seventy years had expired. Perhaps half way through this exile, Daniel became very burdened and longed to see this promised return. He surveyed the spiritual condition of God's people in exile and realized they were terribly guilty of heinous sin. Daniel 9 is a profound prayer, recorded and preserved by the Holy Spirit for our edification. Daniel confesses his own sin and that of God's covenant people. I mentioned this incident in greater detail earlier in this book, but I bring it up again now to urge you to move forward with revival prayer. I focus now on your growth in grace through revival prayer.

Since revival is normative (what God desires, the ten marks of the revival culture found in Acts are the benchmark for every church in every nation) I can go further and say that God wants to bring revival, but we must be willing to pay the price for it.[39] And what is that price? In 2 Chronicles 7:13-14, that well known passage on praying for one's nation, we have the marvelous promise of renewal, revitalization, and revival, positioned in a four-fold conditional context. God is addressing His covenant people during the reign of Solomon, just after the Temple has been dedicated and the Spirit of God has fallen on the people, filling the Temple with the glory of the Lord. A huge sacrificial offering was given to the Lord and the people rejoiced. Afterward Yahweh appears to Solomon in the night, saying that He has heard his prayer, saying that if He shuts up the heavens so that there is no more rain, or if He sends pestilence and as a result His people humble themselves and pray, if they seek His face and turn from their wicked ways, then He promises to hear from heaven, forgive them, and heal their land.

You will note that Yahweh is addressing His covenant people. He says, "and My people who are called by My name." God does not need to hear the fruitless prayers of pagan America to act. He only desires the prayers of His blood bought people, those in covenant with Him, those who have bowed the knee to Jesus, confessing Him alone to be Lord and Savior (Romans 10:9-10).

And what are these four conditions for the restoration of God's favor? First, if God is to heal the land of His people, then they must humble themselves before Him. God is opposed to the proud, but gives grace to the humble. Thus we must humble ourselves under His mighty hand (1 Peter 5:5-6). Isaiah says that God looks to those who are humble and contrite in spirit, who tremble at His word (Isaiah 66:2). He also says that Yahweh dwells in two places, a highly and holy place and with the lowly and contrite of heart to revive the spirit of the lowly and to revive the heart of the contrite (Isaiah 57:15). If God is to move upon us and heal our land, then we, His people, must humble ourselves before Him and our fellow man. O dear people, where shall we begin! We have debased God and exalted ourselves. We have stripped God of His sovereignty by embracing our self-actualization. We have denied the divine authority of His word by exalting our

---

[39]See my devotional *What Is Biblical Revival?* dated February 25, 2010

intellect. We have foolishly rejected all He teaches pertaining to life and godliness in favor of the latest fad coming out of secular universities, main stream media, and Hollywood. We have worshipped the mammon of wealth, trusting it to bring comfort, while rejecting the sufficiency of the Savior who loves us and gave Himself for us. We have grumbled under His frowning providence, forgetting all the while that His blows always are love, that He works all things for good to those who love Him and are called according to His purpose. We, like the church at Thyatira, have tolerated evil in the church and world, failing to confront the wickedness of church and state concerning the sanctity of all human life, sexual perversion in the form of heterosexual and homosexual sin. In cowardice we have listened to the intimidating threats of the world which calls us intolerant for holding these views.

We, like the early church in Jerusalem, have failed to remember that the middle wall of partition has been broken down between Jew and Gentile, that we are guilty of showing personal favoritism to those like us, and rejecting those unlike us ethnically or sociologically. We have failed to deny ourselves sacrificially in all the relationships on which any culture is founded—state, family, church, and business. When in a place of prominence or power, we have not sacrificed, choosing instead to abuse our position by paying ourselves more than we deserve while denying those under us a fair salary. When in a place of submission, we have judged our superiors, assuming they are cheating us, begrudging them their position and income, being guilty of instigating class envy. We have failed to work diligently, robbing our employer while all the while demanding entitlements from him. We have failed to love our wives and children sacrificially, instead choosing to bow the knee to the god of money, position, and fame, sacrificing their spiritual and emotional well being for the mammon we thought would satisfy them. We have worshipped our children, coddled them, failed to demand obedience and hard work from them, being so concerned about their self-esteem that we have crippled them.

We have robbed Christ of His eternal glory by failing to challenge those who mindlessly claim that Jesus is one of many ways to God, that His death and resurrection either did not happen at all or is inconsequential. We have presumed on God, glibly thinking that our programs, personalities, plans, and persuasive powers are sufficient to bring reformation to our culture and church. We have made big ministry plans while forgetting that unless the Lord builds the house, they labor in vain who build it. We have failed to preach Christ crucified, instead offering a psychotherapeutic Jesus who lacks saving and transforming power.

Until we humble ourselves, until we see that we are guilty of heinous sin, until we are profoundly and deeply grieved over our sin, until we see something of the depth of indwelling pride, then we shall not see revival. God resists the proud.

Second, if we are to see revival then we must pray. By prayer I have in mind what we see in the prayer lives of men like Ezra, Nehemiah, Daniel, Jeremiah, Jesus, and Paul. All possessed a God exalting, man debasing spirit. These men prayed long, often, and with earnestness. They labored in prayer. They were relentless. They had faith in God whom they believed would answer them. They prayed alone and they prayed with others. They were focused on Christ and His kingdom. They were decreasing while Jesus was increasing.

By 1744, though pockets of revival were still present in the Great Awakening in America, England, Scotland, and Wales, ministers became alarmed that the revival fires were smoldering. A number of Scottish Presbyterian ministers called for weekly concerts of prayer, either on Saturday evening or Sunday morning. They agreed to pray in this manner for two years. Others soon joined them, including Jonathan Edwards and his church in Northampton, Massachusetts. And what resulted from their prayers? What some church historians call a hidden revival fell upon the British Isles from 1790 to 1840. The Methodist Church, in 1791, the year of John Wesley's death, had 72,000 members. Due to the hidden revival (called this because so few church historians note it, preferring instead to focus on the Great Awakening of 1735 and the 1859 and 1904 revivals), the Methodists had grown, through conversion growth, to over 360,000 by 1850. A total of 1,500,000 people, one in ten, were brought into non-Anglican churches in the British Isles from 1790 to 1840.[40]

Without earnest prayer and without humbling ourselves before God, then we cannot expect revival. But we must also seek God's face. This is part and parcel of the first two components. The Hebrew word for *seek* means to search out, to strive after, to inquire. The same Hebrew word is used extensively in the Psalms. "And those who know Thy name will put their trust in Thee; for Thou, O Lord, hast not forsaken those who seek Thee," (9:10). "The afflicted shall eat and be satisfied; those who seek Him will praise the Lord," (22:26). "He shall receive a blessing from the Lord and righteousness from the God of His salvation. This is the generation of those who seek Him, who seek Thy face— even Jacob," (24:6). "One thing I have asked from the Lord, that I shall seek; that I may dwell in the house of the Lord all the days of my life, to behold the beauty of the Lord, and to meditate in His temple. . . when Thou didst say, 'Seek My face,' my heart said to Thee, 'Thy face, O Lord, I shall seek'" (27:4,8).

To seek God means that we desire Him and His presence more than our necessary food (Isaiah 58:5ff, Matthew 6:16), at times even more than marital, sexual intimacy (1 Corinthians 7:5). It means to hunger and thirst for righteousness (Matthew 5:6, Isaiah 55:1, Psalm 42:1-2). It means that we keep seeking the things above, where Christ is, seated at the right hand of the Father (Colossians 3:1-3). It means that whatever things were gain to us, we count them but rubbish in order that we may gain Christ (Philippians 3:8). It means that we refuse to set our minds on earthly things, remembering that our citizenship is in heaven (Philippians 3:19-20).

To seek the face of God is difficult in any historical and cultural context but modernity presents us with our own set of problems in this regard. The noise, the pace of life, all our technology constantly work to mitigate a zeal for God. Instead of coming in at night after a meeting and spending time with a good book, I tend to turn on the television and fritter away an hour or two before going to bed. Sometimes a television program particularly grabs my attention and I stay up too late at night, and do not get up early enough in the morning to spend lengthy time with God. And sometimes while meeting with God in the early morning hours I suddenly remember someone I "must" contact and quickly open my e mail account. The next thing I know I have wasted an hour of valuable "God time" on lesser things like e-mail correspondence or reading my favorite on-line newspaper.

We do not seek the face of God because we are not desperate for holiness and revival. A man who has not had water in three days can think of nothing but getting water. He would pay any sum demanded to have that water because he knows it is a matter of life and death. A couple whose ten year old daughter is missing will pray earnestly, stay up all night, follow every lead, pay any sum required to get back their daughter. They are

---

[40] *Give Him No Rest*, Erroll Hulse, pages 97-100.

desperate. We are not desperate for revival because we are not overly concerned with the glory of God, His weightiness, His manifold attributes being displayed to a world of scoffers. We have our own salvation and that typically is enough for us. We are not grieved by the few numbers of converts we see in our churches. Perhaps we have comforted ourselves by wrongly applying the doctrine of election, thinking that the few conversions we see must be God's eternal plan, failing to understand that we have no idea how many elect there are, failing to keep in mind that God's benchmark is the book of Acts, that we ought to be seeing many conversions everywhere. Perhaps our lack of zeal for God, coupled with our natural cowardice, has convinced us that better days have passed us by, that God's great work today is limited to what World Mission experts call the southern world of China, South America, and Africa.

What does it look like to seek God? This is not easy to quantify or qualify. We cannot simply put a measure of hours per day one spends alone in earnest prayer, though surely this must require some substantial investment of time. A man who says that he loves his wife but rarely sits down to talk with her, who refuses to spend anytime with her, betrays his own profession. A man who says that quality of time with his children is more important than quantity of time is only half right. One may desire a filet mignon of excellent quality but at the same time he expects it to be larger and weightier than a postage stamp. To seek God's face begins with a heartfelt desperation—a hunger and thirst for holiness, a zeal for the glory of God in the salvation and sanctification of sinners. There will be fervency, persistence, earnestness in prayer that will surely translate into longer times with God than one previously experienced. How long? I don't know. It will vary from person to person.

And if we are to see revival today, not only must we humble ourselves, pray, and seek the face of God, but we must also turn from our wicked ways. Remember—God is not saying that our wicked, unregenerate culture must turn from her wicked ways. The emphasis is on the people of God—"If *My* people, who are called by *My* name . . . "

Evan Roberts, the leader of the Welsh revival of 1904, 1905 told the people that they must do four things to see revival. One, past sins must be confessed or the Spirit will not come. Two, anything doubtful (possibly displeasing to God) must be removed. Three, they must obey immediately any promptings of the Holy Spirit. And four, new converts must make a public confession of Christ as Lord and Savior.[41] The consequent revival was copious and profound.

A revival fell in 1974 upon the Baptist Church in Oradea, Romania. Romania was perhaps the most oppressed of all the Eastern bloc countries and the church was mired in scandalous, godless behavior and lethargy. Pastor Livu Olah called for repentance and began preaching with great power. Within minutes after he began his sermons the people were weeping over their sin, heartbroken, ready to forsake their evil ways. This spread throughout the congregation and conversions began to multiply. By June, 1974 one hundred converts had been baptized. By the end of 1974, another two hundred and forty-nine were baptized, with one hundred and forty-nine coming in one service alone.[42]

---

[41] *The Welsh Revival of 1904*, Eifion Evans, Page 84.

[42] *Give Him No Rest*, Erroll Hulse, page 136.

Something similar happened in 1907 in Pyongyang, Korea. After ten years of ministry in the 1880's by Presbyterian missionaries from America, there were only seventy-four Protestants in the entire country. By 1930 there were 415,000, and by 1955 there were 1,170,000.[43] Today one in four South Koreans are Christians. How did this happen? It began with a men's prayer meeting at Pyongyang when the Holy Spirit came upon the assembly, bringing a deep conviction of sin, resulting in a prolonged time of agony and repentance, causing them to make right the wrongs each had done to one another. Those who had stolen goods returned them. Those who had held grudges confessed and sought reconciliation. The spirit of repentance, of turning from their wicked ways, spread throughout the church in Korea. Unbelievers in huge numbers began to be saved. And when persecution came at the hands of the Japanese, the American Presbyterian missionaries stayed with their Korean brethren, not fleeing to safety, and suffered death with them.[44]

And what does it mean today for us to turn from our wicked ways? If we are to see revival then we must ask God to show us our own sin, to ransack our hearts and minds (Psalm 139:23-24). As God the Holy Spirit shows us our sin, then we must be quick to confess it to God and to others (James 5:16). Perhaps there is so much sin, packed deeply into our lives, that we are not even aware of it, not sensitive to it. We must ask the Holy Spirit to give us tender consciences and hearts, the humility to admit our sins to one another. How frightening! We all want to look good, to appear spiritual before our friends and peers. Some today flippantly confess their sins without any apparent desire to hate them and forsake them, but when the Spirit comes there is a holy hatred and grief over sin, an earnest desire to turn from it. Certainly wisdom ought to be used in having public confession where those of the opposite sex may be present. These are delicate matters which the Elders of the church must carefully govern. Furthermore, this is not something that should be contrived or manipulated. All sin, any sin must come under the purview of the Holy Spirit, and when revealed, must be confessed, repented of, and forsaken.

May God so work in our churches, in our leadership, that He moves upon His people to humble themselves and to pray, to seek the face of God, and to forsake our wicked ways. He then promises to forgive us and to heal our land. These are the requirements for a return to the revival salvation of the book of Acts and this alone will prevail in our modern world where we know so little gospel power.

There are four more living stones of revival prayer, necessary to construct our churches as houses of prayer for the nations. In following through on what I just wrote concerning 2 Chronicles 7:14, we must learn to pray in holiness, faith, fervency, and urgency. Now, what do I mean by these four terms? First, we are to pray in holiness. King David tells us that if we regard iniquity in our heart, then the Lord will not hear us (Psalm 66:18). Isaiah, in preaching to Israel and Judah around 730 B.C., says, "The arm of the Lord is not so short that it cannot save, nor is His ear so dull that it cannot hear, but your iniquities have made a separation between you and your God, and your sins have hid His face from you," (Isaiah 59:1-2). While it is certainly true that God loves His people with an everlasting love, that He has removed our sins from us as far as the east is from the west, that we now have peace with God through our Lord Jesus Christ, that there is no

---

[43] Ibid. page 138.

[44] See the *The Korean Pentecost and the Suffering Which Followed*, by William Blair and Bruce Hunt, published by Banner of Truth, for a remarkable example of revival.

longer any condemnation for those who are in Christ Jesus, that nothing shall ever be able to separate us from the love of God which is in Christ Jesus our Lord; it is also true that our sins grieve and quench the Holy Spirit (Ephesians 4:30, 1 Thessalonians 5:19), that God is angry with us in our sin, that He will chastise those who are His (Revelation 3:19, Hebrews 12:10-11). Think of it this way, I love my wife dearly and she loves me. We have been married for nearly forty years, and we are not contemplating divorce. Nevertheless, there have been many times when I have offended or hurt her by my words or actions. So, when I come home at night, after I have hurt her, the house feels like a meat locker. It's very cold in the house! In other words, though we love each other and we are committed to each other, a wall of separation stands between us in our relationship. So what must I do? I must acknowledge my sin to her, apologize, ask her forgiveness, and promise, by God's grace, not to do it again. And she readily forgives me. We are reconciled, and we move forward. Now that's how it is with God. He loves you in Christ. He is committed to you, but your sin has brought a separation between you and Him. You must repent and come back to Him.

So a vital ingredient of revival prayer, of making your church a house of prayer for the nations is for you and your fellow church members to walk in Biblical holiness. Be sure of this—you have no holiness in yourself, no more than you have the righteousness that merits your justification. Jesus is your holiness (1 Corinthians 1:30). You must run to Him, wrap your arms around Him, as it were, and ask Him for His holiness. Here's another analogy. Let's say you are at a picnic on a beautiful summer day, and you are playing ball with your children when all of a sudden, a swarm of bees attacks you, stinging you unceasingly. You cannot find relief so you run down to the river in the nearby meadow, with the bees still following and stinging you, and you plunge yourself under the water. The bees then relent. As long as you stay under the water, the bees do not attack you. When you sin, the law of God stings you (1 Corinthians 15:56) and the pain of this sting drives the believer to Jesus for refuge. You are to run to the river, as it were, filled with the blood of Jesus and the sanctifying water of the Holy Spirit. As you keep yourself plunged under the sanctifying presence of the Spirit, all is well with you. The moment you come out from under the living and sanctifying water of the Spirit is the moment you have trouble again. If I cut off the top and bottom of a two liter soft drink bottle, how will it be able again to hold water? The only way is to keep the bottle submerged under the water. So it is with us in Christ Jesus. You continue in gospel holiness only as you hold onto Jesus, as you grab hold of His holiness, as you keep yourself submerged under His gracious presence, as you abide in Him who alone makes possible fruit bearing (John 15:1-5).

And beyond this, if you are to engage in revival prayer, if your church is to become a house of prayer to the nations, then you must pray in faith. The writer to the Hebrews tells us that without faith it is impossible to please God, that those who come to Him must believe that He is, that He rewards those who diligently seek Him (Hebrews 11:6). Jesus said, "Whatever you ask in prayer, believing you shall receive (Matthew 21:22). He also said, "Ask and you shall receive. Seek and you shall find. Knock and the door shall be opened to you. For he asks, receives. He who seeks, finds. And he who knocks, the door is opened to him, (Matthew 7:7-8). Jesus drives home this vital truth even further by arguing the greater to the lesser. He says, "If a son asks a father for bread, he will not give him a stone, will he? If a son asks for a fish, the father will not give him a snake, will he? If you, being evil, know how to give good gifts to your children, how much more will your Father give good things to those who ask Him (Matthew 7:9-11). I always marvel at how we so easily dismiss these glorious promises. Our young children have no trouble at all believing God's promises. No wonder Jesus told us that we are to be as children if we are to enter the kingdom of heaven (Matthew 18:3-4, 19:14).

I remember at a former church, one of our missionaries asking that we pray God would give him a wife. Unbeknownst to me, two little boys in our church, age five, began praying nightly for this young man, that God would grant him a wife. Two years later the missionary calls me and tells me that he was soon to be married. I said to him, "You must call these two little boys. They have been praying daily for you."

My friends, we have not because we ask not. Perhaps you object and say, "Now wait a minute. Does praying in faith mean that I can ask God for $1 million and I will get it? Does it mean I can ask for a new Mercedes and get it? That sounds like health and wealth gospel heresy." Keep in mind all we have said thus far about prayer. We must pray with the heart of Jesus, in the name of Jesus. We must pray the word of God for that is His will. We must pray in the Spirit. We must pray in gospel holiness. When the Bible says, "Whatever you ask in prayer believing, you will receive," keep in mind the context, the conditions of prayer just mentioned. Think of it this way—if I go to a nice restaurant with my wife, and the waiter asks, "Is everything okay, sir?" We instinctively know that he is not asking me "How is your marriage? How is your health? How is your 401k?" He is asking "In the context of this dining experience, how is everything? How is the food? How is the service? How is the ambience of the restaurant?"

If we pray with all these previously mentioned living stones in place, then we should ask in faith, simply believing that God will answer us, just like a child who never doubts that his father will provide the evening meal, a place to sleep, and the clothing he needs.

So, my friend, are you keeping short accounts concerning gospel holiness? When you see your sin, are you quick to confess it and repent of it? Are you sensitive to your sin? Does it grieve you? Are you zealous to make things right with God and those whom you have hurt by your sin? And do you believe God? After all, why do you pray? Are you simply taking up time during your day, or are you expectant? It seems to me that many in our evangelical churches simply do not believe much is to happen in their lives, families, or churches. We should ask expectantly, with faith, expecting God to answer.

And then you must pray with fervency. In Psalm 63 King David is on the run, in the wilderness. We cannot tell if it was when he was fleeing King Saul or if it was later when he was fleeing his son, Absalom, who had usurped the kingdom from him. At any rate, he is in dire straits. And it is within this dreadful context that he cries out, "O God, Thou art my God. I will seek Thee earnestly. My soul longs for Thee. My flesh yearns for Thee, in a dry and weary land where there is no water. Thus I have seen Thee in the sanctuary, to see Thy power and Thy glory," (Psalm 63:1-2). David, due to his hardship, prays with fervency. Is it not true that too often are prayers are offered in a perfunctory fashion, merely going through the motions, simply praying to "check this duty off our list." But when God gives you the intolerable burden for your own sin, for the lukewarmness and the loss of your first love; when you come to understand more fully the insipid nature of the church, our impotence and inability to affect change in our culture, when you come to understand the church's disenfranchisement; when your heart begins to break for the children gunned down in our schools, for the hopelessness of so many in our inner cities, when you begin to realize that Islam is knocking on the door of our western civilization, zealously committed to Shariah Law, then you will pray with fervency. You cannot be lackadaisical in such matters. So, are you praying with fervency, or are you simply paying lip service to prayer?

And finally, you must pray with urgency. This differs from fervency. How so? In Isaiah 64:1-2, as Israel is facing invasion by the wicked nation of Assyria, as Judah later faces the same judgment at the hands of the Babylonian empire, as Isaiah has repeatedly pronounced judgment on recalcitrant Israel and Judah, he now prays, "O, that Thou wouldst rend the heavens and come down, that the mountains might quake at Thy presence—As fire kindles the brushwood, as fire causes the water to boil—to make Thy name known to Thine adversaries, that the nations may tremble at Thy presence." Isaiah prays with urgency. He is asking for God's palpable presence of power to intervene on behalf of His people. He is asking God to rip open heaven and to come down, to show Himself mighty in the presence of His enemies. Those who have experienced an earthquake, who have seen the ground tremble, are awed by the manifestation of such power. Isaiah earnestly and urgently wants to see this in a spiritual fashion. When a forest fire rages through a forest, it first burns off the brushwood. In fact farmers often have "controlled burnings" of forests, to burn off the brushwood, to enable the trees to reach their full stature more easily. And as fire causes water to boil, so Isaiah wants to see God come with such power to turn lukewarm, room temperature water into a raging, boiling cauldron. When the Holy Spirit comes down in such presence and power, the "brushwood" that so easily entangles us—things like chronic marital or familial problems; division, strife, and unresolved conflict in the church or family; emotional, spiritual, or psychological problems of parishioners that have long resisted even the best of counselors' intervention, are suddenly swept away by the power of the Spirit's presence. All our adversaries fall before us when the Spirit comes down.

My brethren, is this not a time for urgency in prayer? Are we not in tempestuous times? Business as usual is not working, is it? We must have the unction, the anointing of the Holy Spirit upon our ministries. The time is now. We need the Spirit now in great power. Pray, my friends, with a deep, abiding sense of urgency.

Part III: MAKING YOUR CHURCH A HOUSE OF PRAYER FOR THE NATIONS

Chapter 8
Outwardly, Stressing the Need of Community

John Girardeau, of French Huguenot descent, was born at James Island, near Charleston, SC in 1825 and was reared on the *Westminster Confession of Faith* and the *Shorter and Larger Catechism*. His mother died when he was seven years old and he says he felt the heavy price of tuition in the school of affliction. He enrolled at the College of Charleston at the age of fifteen and was still, at the time, unconverted. While in his first year of college, Girardeau suffered under a month long profound conviction of sin that took away his appetite and caused him to seek God earnestly for the forgiveness of his sins. He feared falling asleep at night lest he wake up in hell. However, after reading John Calvin, John Owen, and Thomas Halyburton the Holy Spirit gave him a sense of his forgiveness in Christ. From that point forward Girardeau lived with an overwhelming sense of the joy of salvation, compassion for the lost and suffering humanity, and a burden to preach the unsearchable riches of Christ. After his graduation from the College of Charleston he enrolled in Columbia Theological Seminary of the Presbyterian Church to become a minister of the gospel. He studied under the great Southern Presbyterian preacher and theologian James Henley Thornwell and attended First Presbyterian Church, Columbia, SC and listened to the equally gifted preacher Benjamin Palmer. He did not wait until his graduation to minister the gospel in difficult places. He regularly went to the wharf areas of Charleston and evangelized the unwashed peoples there, including a number of prostitutes who made professions of faith. His great burden, however, was the low country black slaves in that region of South Carolina. There was very little gospel witness among them, and when he married his wife, Penelope Sarah Hamlin, in 1849, though both came from the privilege of plantation life, their hearts were with the black slaves. Upon graduation from Columbia Seminary, Girardeau was the supply preacher for a number of small congregations in rural South Carolina, outside of Charleston; and God used him powerfully to preach, both to the slaves and the white people there. Meanwhile the Second Presbyterian Church of Charleston wanted to plant a church with their black slave members and asked Girardeau to be their church planter. He agreed and began his ministry in 1851 with thirty members. By 1860 the church, Zion Presbyterian Church on Calhoun Street, had six hundred members (all but about ten percent were black slaves) and a regular Sunday attendance of over 1500. The congregation built the largest structure in Charleston and possibly in all of South Carolina at the time. While the slaves were illiterate, they nonetheless were taught the *Shorter Catechism* of the *Westminster Confession of Faith*. Girardeau also developed a method of dividing his congregation into groups of forty which were led by slaves who shepherded the people.[45]

But what I wish to emphasize was Girardeau's commitment to his rich Southern Presbyterian theological tradition. This commitment flowed from the recovery of the doctrines of grace (the five *sola*s of the Reformation—*sola scriptura*, s*ola fide, sola gratia, solus Christus, soli deo gloria)* of the sixteenth century, led by Martin Luther, John Calvin, and John Knox; the intellectual and theological precision of the seventeenth century Puritan revolution which birthed the *Westminster Confession of Faith,* and the

---

[45] For important details on Girardeau's life and ministry, as well as those of several other great nineteenth century Presbyterian preachers, see Douglas Kelly's wonderful book *Preachers with Power: Four Stalwarts of the South.*

experiential, heart-felt, Spirit anointed Great Awakening of the eighteenth century, as well as the God-centered, nineteenth century Second Great Awakening led by men like Asahel Nettleton. In other words, Girardeau's ministry was founded on experiential Calvinism. His was not a dry as dust, cerebral approach to ministry. He preached the doctrines of grace with theological precision, adapting these great truths to his hearers, all the while looking to the Holy Spirit's anointing to break the hearts of the unconverted, driving them to Jesus for refuge, and strengthening the hearts of the redeemed to look to their great union with Christ as the means of comfort and sanctification.

By 1857 Jeremiah Lamphier, in the midst of a terrible recession and stock market crash, called the people of New York City to pray for revival. By October of that year 10,000 people were meeting on their lunch hour in Manhattan to pray. God poured out His Spirit, resulting in a mighty prayer movement that swept over the United States and moved to Scotland, Wales, Northern Ireland, and Hawaii, ushering an estimated one million people into the kingdom of God. Girardeau's members heard of God's great revival and asked if they could meet regularly to pray for the same visitation on their church and city. He agreed and they began praying nightly at the church. He was asked to preach each night but refused, instead believing that they should wait for the Spirit's visitation. One night, after they had been praying for several weeks, as Girardeau was leading his congregation in the closing hymn (they sang *A Capella*, don't you wish you could have heard that glorious singing!) he felt a sensation, like a bolt of electricity, flowing from his head through his entire body. He knew the Spirit had come. He pronounced the benediction to his standing congregation, informing them that he would begin preaching the next night. The congregation all sat down at once. Girardeau then realized the Spirit had come upon them as well. So he began exhorting them to repent and believe the gospel. At first there was light weeping over sin, then came a torrent of tears and confession, crying out to God for mercy. Others were weeping tears of joy at having been delivered from death to life, from the dominion of sin to newness of life in Christ. The preaching continued nightly for seven weeks. Hundreds, both black slaves and white people, were converted. Just a few years later, many of the young white men who were born again in the revival would die on the battlefields of the War Between the States. Brethren, we must have a similar revival or we are doomed, and that revival will only come through similar prayer.

We now address the four last living stones which compose the house of prayer for the nations. While the first four are concerned with our relationship with God, and while the second four address our own personal growth in holiness, these last four emphasize the covenant community of believers. First, we pray with humility. I have already emphasized, in some detail, the vital necessity of contrition and repentance, and I said that we must ask the Holy Spirit to show us our sin of pride, unbelief, and rebellion. God is opposed to the proud, but gives grace to the humble (1 Peter 5:5). We see this plainly illustrated in the life of King David after his adultery and the murder of Bathsheba's husband, Uriah the Hittite. It appears that David went on in an unrepentant state for some time, perhaps as much as one year, but then Nathan painted a vivid picture for him, one that grabbed his heart and drove him to his knees in evangelical repentance (2 Samuel 12:13, Psalm 51, 32). It is within this context that David wrote Psalm 51, a marvelous lament over his sin and his consequent repentance. David wrote, "A broken and contrite heart, O God, Thou wilt not despise," (Psalm 51:17). One of the most practical ways to pray in humility is to engage in accountability with other believers of the same sex. In James 5:16, in the context of praying for one who is sick, James writes, "Therefore, confess your sins to one another, and pray for one another that you may be healed. The effective, fervent prayer of a righteous man accomplishes much." He then illustrates this kind of fervent and effective prayer by citing Elijah, a man with passions like ours, but who, nonetheless, prayed earnestly that it would not rain during the days of Ahab and Jezebel; and it did not rain for three years and six months. Then he prayed again and the sky poured forth rain and the earth produced its fruit (James 5:17-18). Here's what I mean by accountability. While pastoring a church in Connecticut I met weekly with two other brothers in the Lord, men who were not members of the church I served. We agreed that we could ask each other anything about our walks with the Lord, our struggles with sin, how things were going in our marriages, etc. And we did. Dietrich Bonhoeffer in his book, *Life Together,* wonders if we are really confessing our sins to God if we are not doing so with other brothers and sisters in the Lord.[46] That's because when we merely confess our sins to God we tend to go back to them fairly easily, but when we confess to others, it is much more difficult to continue in them. Why? Because we know we will see those brothers in a few days and they are going to ask us the hard questions. There is something very humbling about admitting to others who love you that you have a particular struggle with a particular sin.

So I urge you to find a small, accountability group with whom you meet weekly and give each other the permission to ask you the hard, sin questions. Be careful, however. I heard of a pastor who told his elders that a couple of women in the congregation were tempting him as he preached because they were dressed inappropriately. One of the elders mentioned this to his wife, and word spread like wildfire that the preacher was lusting after these church women. Needless to say his ministry was over in short order at that church. And confessing such sensitive, even sensual sin in mixed company is a no no. Be prudent where you confess your sins, but you do need to confess them somewhere, to somebody. And when you confess them you must truly grieve over your sins. It is very easy to impugn God's grace and mercy by taking lightly our sin. Jesus said, "Blessed are those who mourn, for they shall be comforted," (Matthew 5:4). James said, "Be miserable, mourn, and weep. Let your laughter be turned to sorrow and your joy to gloom," (James 4:9). At the same time we are to rejoice in the Lord always (Philippians 3:1, 4:4). So, which is it? Are we to rejoice or are we to grieve? The answer is, "Yes." We are to do both at the same time. As you truly grieve over your sin, as you see more clearly how you have sinned against such marvelous grace, then your grief will be turned to joy when you contemplate something of the height and depth and breadth and length of the love of God in Christ Jesus (Ephesians 3:18-19, Romans 8:35-39).

But then you also are to pray in unity. Jesus takes this up in Matthew 18:19. He promises that agreement on earth brings God's action in heaven. This, of course, is no more a *carte blanche* promise than is "Whatever you ask in prayer believing, you will receive." There is a context here that we must keep in mind. In Matthew 18 Jesus is dealing with believers living righteously in the church. He says that we are to be like children, humbling ourselves (verses 3-4). He warns us against being a stumbling block to little children (verses 5-11). He reminds us that the purpose of the church is to leave the ninety-nine who are already in the fold and go find the wandering sheep (verses 12-14). Then He takes up the issue of a brother or sister sinning against us, giving us the proper procedure in addressing their sin (verses 15-18). Finally, within this context Jesus says that if two agree on earth about anything then it shall be done for them by our Father who is in heaven (verse 19). Jesus is all about unity in the body of Christ, walking humbly before one another, giving each other the benefit of the doubt, forgiving each other seventy times seven. In other words, unity in the body of Christ is absolutely essential to

---

[46] *Life Together,* page

God answering prayer. With unity we can be sure that our prayers will be answered, provided we are holding to the other living stones about which we have already written.

If there is disunity in your church body, if there is unresolved conflict, if people are sowing seeds of discord among the brethren, if the pastor or elders are being spiritually abusive, if the congregants are spiritually abusing the pastor or elders, if there is anything in the local body that smacks of rebellions, dragging the bride of Christ, through the mud, as it were, then you be sure of this—you are not agreeing on earth, and because of this, you will not have from the Father what you have requested.

Here's my example—let's say that I came to preach at your church and I brought one of my youngest grandchildren with me, and planned to place him in the nursery during the service. As I entered the nursery, however, I noticed several of the infants with green mucus coming out their noses. I now realize these children are sick and I therefore refuse to place my grandchild in the nursery. Why? Because there is sickness there and I love my grandchild too much to expose him unnecessarily to sickness. How much more so, my dear friend, does God love His little lambs, those who have just entered into the kingdom through regeneration? And how much more than us does He love those who are seeking after Christ but are not yet born again? If there is unresolved division and strife in your church then God will keep His "little ones" from your church. He will send them elsewhere.

I remember sadly this very thing happening in one of my early ministries. I handled our Administrative Assistant harshly and she rebelled, sowing strife and discord among the saints. It was awful. The church, up until that point, was a loving, caring, and growing congregation. Afterwards, however, it was as though the Holy Spirit took a vacation. He was not there. We still had our ministries going. I still preached. We still discipled. We still evangelized, but with little power. Eventually, the church shrank almost to nothing. Is there strife, division, or discord in your church? You must deal with it biblically. Until you do, God will resist you. You will not be praying in unity, and thus you will not see Holy Spirit power on the ministry.

And then you must pray with community. After the issue of unity, Jesus then says, "For where two or three have gathered together in My name, I am there in their midst," (Matthew 18:20). While it is certainly vital to pray privately in your own daily devotional time, and while it is also important for the congregation to engage in corporate prayer in the worship service or during a mid-week prayer meeting, it is powerfully effective to pray with a small group of believers. I urge you to find at least four other believers with whom you can pray weekly, for at least one hour, per week for revival prayer. This must be the real work for any church which longs to see a mighty movement of God in their community. When my wife and I went to Connecticut to plant the church we knew that only one percent of the state was evangelical. We knew that the people there were not "buying" what we were selling. I told our small core group that we must build the church on prayer and evangelism. So we began with a couple of all night prayer meetings. These were okay but it is hard to sustain those over a long period of time. Then we tried once per month, on Friday nights, from eight p.m. to midnight. I like to make it difficult for people to come to prayer meetings! We did that for a year or so but then finally settled on Sunday nights, after our evening activities, at our house, from 7:30 to 9:00 p.m. I let our people know that we would not be taking prayer requests. You know how that typically goes. People engage in "organ recitals" (praying for Aunt Matilda's bunion) or travelogues (Lord please grant Jerry traveling mercies this week on his trip) for forty-five minutes, pray for ten minutes, and then go home. So, I said, "Here's what we are going to do. We are going to pray for four things—the lost by name, that they will come to know Jesus as their Lord and Savior; revival, that God will pour out His Spirit with a mighty movement that will transform our community and nation; for our missionaries, their particular needs, the progress of the gospel in their locales; and for church planting and church revitalization." So we typically gathered in our kitchen and drank coffee or tea for fifteen minutes and then made our way into our living room and prayed for more than hour. We always concluded promptly at 9 p.m. This was the lifeblood of our church. Those with whom we prayed were our closest friends. There is something powerful when like-minded believers come together before the throne of grace concerning His business. There was profound unity and love for one another.

Here's another reason why praying in community is important. I have noticed, in my own prayer life, that my flesh does everything possible not to pray. Has this been your experience? It is truly shocking to me. There are many times I simply do not want to pray privately. I will think of every other thing to do, even good things, like reading the Bible or a good Christian book; but to pray is exceedingly difficult. In fact, I have prayed for several hours at a time with other believers, and I doubt that I could do that by myself. That's the beauty of community in prayer!

You see, prayer is the most intimate spiritual exercise anyone can do, and if there is division and strife, then people will not pray together. When I talk with a couple having marital problems the first question I ask them is, "Do you pray regularly together?" The answer always is, "No." Why? Because those hostile toward each other will avoid such spiritual intimacy. In like manner, to pray with other brothers and sisters will require you to keep short accounts, to work through your differences. Have you noticed how the greatest generation, our World War II veterans would annually meet for their reunions. Why? They went through things, saw things, did things with which most of us cannot identify. They were in the battle together. Those with whom my wife and I prayed every Sunday night were fellow warriors. There was a closeness with them that was wonderful, and we miss it terribly.

So, do you have a small group with which you can prayer regularly? If not, find one, and give yourself to revival prayer.

And finally, learn to pray with persistence. In 1 Thessalonians 5:17, within the context of numerous commands, the Apostle Paul writes, "Pray without ceasing." Now, what does this mean? Many have speculated. Here's my take. Paul means at least two things. First, to pray without ceasing means to pray without thought as to the time. There have been many times, in our Days of Revival Prayer when we pray for twelve hours, that the time has flown by. Typically the actual prayer sessions last three hours. When we are praying in the Spirit we are unaware of the time. And second, to pray without ceasing means you pray until you receive an answer. If you are praying for someone's salvation, you continue to pray until the person is saved or he dies. Isn't that what Jesus is after when He teaches us about importunity in prayer (Luke 11:5-8)? The friend who knocks on your door at midnight, asking for three loaves of bread, will not go away until you get up out of bed and give him what he requests. Jesus is telling us that we are to be shameless in our requests. He is our loving Savior, the One who always intercedes for us. Don't give up. Don't quit. Persevere. Be persistent in prayer. If you are praying for one's healing, then pray until you receive your answer—either the person is healed or he dies! Pray with persistence for revival. I have people ask me all the time, "Do you believe that God will bring revival to America?" My answer is, "I don't know, but our job is to pray. We are to be like David when his son by Bathsheba was sick. He prayed, fasted, sought God earnestly for seven days for his son's healing. When his son died, his entourage was afraid to tell him, but David sensed what had happened. He got up, washed his face, anointed himself, changed his clothes, and went into the house of the Lord. In other words, he went on with his life (2 Samuel 12:15-20). Our job is to do the same thing concerning revival."

After my conversion in college I began to pray for my parents and siblings. I am sure I was harsh in those early days in how I sought to win them to Christ. Consequently there was no small degree of alienation in our family concerning my new found faith. However, over the years my family members have come to Christ. I have been praying for forty years now! Be persistent. Don't give up. Persevere.

The great man of faith, George Mueller, was known for God's mighty answers to prayer on his behalf. The stories are many and thrilling. Mueller kept a diary of his prayer requests, especially of friends for whom he was praying for their salvation. Upon his death, all but two of Mueller's friends had been converted over the years. So what happened to the two who were not yet converted? Within a year or two these also came into the kingdom of God!

I am after one thing—that your church may become a house of prayer for the nations. We are in big trouble in the church of Jesus. Business as usual is not working. We need a major paradigm shift. I am challenging you to begin revival prayer meetings in your church, meetings of at least five people who meet for at least an hour each week in revival prayer. This requires a major shift in your thinking. I am not suggesting you try this idea of revival prayer for a few months, and if it does not bear fruit, you abandon it, like we tend to do with programs that don't work. No, this is revival prayer. We are desperate. We are like the Syrophonecian woman in Mark 7 whose daughter is demon possessed. The woman has tried everything, but to no avail. She hears of Jesus healing and casting out demons. In her desperation she is hopeful. She goes to Jesus, falls before Him, continually beseeching Him for His favor. At first Jesus puts her off, saying, "It is not good to give the children's food to dogs." The Jews viewed Gentiles, like this woman, as less than human. But the woman is persistent. She will not give up. She continues to seek Jesus' favor by saying, "Yes, that's true, but even dogs ought to be able to eat crumbs from the master's table." Jesus rewards her humble, persistent faith by healing her daughter.

My friend, we are desperate but we should also be hopeful. There is always hope in Jesus! So, commit yourself to revival prayer. Get your small group of four other believers and begin right away. Use what you have read, thus far, to begin revival prayer. I will follow now with specific, practical ways in which you can engage in revival prayer.

Part IV: PRACTICALLY, HOW DO WE DO REVIVAL PRAYER?

Chapter 9
A Weekend of Revival Prayer

Okay, I have laid out the necessity for an intolerable burden and contrition and repentance as the vital foundation for revival prayer. Then I defined revival in three ways. First I did so exegetically, as we looked at a brief exposition of Psalm 85. Next we studied this historically, looking at the history of revivals, seeking to make clear the elements of them in church history. Finally we looked at the issue of revival topically. There I stated the ten marks of a revival culture, drawing them from the book of Acts. Next we spent a great deal of time on making the church a house of prayer for the nations. We looked briefly, again, at the twin pillars of the intolerable burden and contrition leading to repentance. Then I laid out the twelve living stones which make up a house of prayer for the nations. But now the question is—how do we actually engage in revival prayer?

We begin with the premise that we should devote twelve hours to revival prayer, right at the beginning. After hearing that Israel was giving their children to be married to pagans, Ezra sat down appalled until the evening offering, and then got up in humiliation, tore his garments, fell on his knees, stretched out his hands to the Lord and pulled the hair out of his head and beard (Ezra 9:5-6). In similar fashion, Daniel, after reading the prophet Jeremiah on the prophesied return from the exile within seventy years, confesses the sins of God's covenant people. Afterward, in his extreme weariness, the angel Gabriel came to Daniel at the evening offering (Daniel 9:21). It appears, therefore, that both Ezra and Daniel had been devoting themselves all day to prayer, manifesting this intolerable burden which we must all have if we are to see a mighty movement of God in our day.

So with that in mind, we typically begin our twelve hours of prayer on a Friday night, from 6 p.m. to 10 p.m. We gather everyone together and I speak for an hour to ninety minutes of the intolerable burden and contrition leading to repentance. I also state upfront that our objective, by the end of the weekend, is to have at least one group of five people in the church engaged in revival prayer for one hour per week. This is a paradigm shift. We are challenging people to commit to revival prayer from that point forward. I explain that we are here to learn how to pray more effectively. I will teach on what we mean by revival prayer. I will teach on how to do it, and I will model it for the people. They will be given opportunity to pray in the small groups. I stress that this is not a competition. We are not there to impress anyone, so no one needs to feel intimidated or "out gunned." We put the chairs in a circle and I begin praying. I purposely pray for an extended time, between thirty and sixty minutes. That's because I want people to get a feel for what we mean by revival prayer. I encourage the person to my right to pray next. We continue around the circle until all have had an opportunity to pray. This first prayer session usually takes up to three hours. If everyone prays and we still have time left over, then I will pray again and we will go around the circle again. By the end of the first session, it is time to go home.

We return the next morning and have two more sessions of revival prayer—one from 8 a.m. to noon and the other from noon to 4 p.m. Sometimes we fast, sometimes we do not. It depends on what the pastor and leaders want to do. We realize some are unable to fast due to medical concerns, and some simply do not want to do so. This issue should not deter anyone from coming to the prayer meeting. If we do have food, we suggest light food—fruits, nuts, water, coffee, etc. The second and third sessions are similar. We follow the same format. I teach, in the second session, on the ten marks of the revival culture. I also usually take up the material on making your church a house of prayer for the nations, usually making it through the first four living stones in this lecture. We then pray as we did the night before. The prayer time usually lasts for three hours. And in the third and final session I teach on the last eight living stones of making your church a house of prayer for the nations. We usually end the last session a few minutes before 4 p.m. so that we can briefly share what we have learned. By the way, if I have someone with me who has led in these weekends of revival prayer, then I have them take half the group, and I take the rest. If the group is less than ten people, then we are able to stay in one group the entire time. Anything more than ten people, and we like to divide into at least two groups. I usually stay over the next day and preach the morning worship service and teach in an adult Sunday School class (sometimes the elders decide to combine adult classes) so that I may summarize and reinforce all that I taught the two previous days.

Weekly Revival Prayer

So, after a weekend of revival prayer, then what? We encourage churches to begin weekly revival prayer meetings that last for at least one hour. Some churches incorporate this into a regular Wednesday night program. Some groups, especially men's groups, often meet early in the morning before work. Women who are at home with children, or who work outside the home, often find a weekday night for their revival prayer meeting. That way their husbands can be home with the children while they are out at the prayer meeting. I encourage the people to learn to pray for longer, more extended periods of time. Conversational prayer, or praying a sentence or two, is certainly okay, but we hope to see people graduate to more extended, more substantive praying. As I mentioned earlier, our revival prayer group at our former church met weekly and prayed for sixty to seventy-five minutes and we did not take prayer requests. We all knew the four things for which we were to pray—for the salvation of the lost; for revival in our church, community, and nation; for our missionaries; and for church planting and church revitalization. So, we just began praying and God always showed up with great power. You may wish to consult the material in the appendix "How to Pray in the Church" for very practical help on varying your prayer times. There is a great deal of information there.

Staying at It

How do we stay at it? How do we maintain a revival prayer ministry in the church? After all, we all can become easily side-tracked into lesser things. We can become discouraged if we are not seeing much happen. And we all grow cold and hard-hearted at times. What can you do to persevere in revival prayer? Consider the words of the writer to the Hebrews. He is writing to second generation Jewish believers who are potentially going back to Judaism. He takes two different approaches in seeking to "keep them in the fold." At times he reminds them of the excellency of Jesus over Moses, angels, man, and high priests (Hebrews 1:4ff, 2:5ff, 3:1ff). At other times he warns them of the dire consequences of turning away from the Lord (Hebrews 4:1ff, 6:1ff, 10:19-39, 12:18-29). And he says in Hebrews 3:12-14, "Take care, brethren, that there not be in any one of you an evil, unbelieving heart that falls away from the living God. But encourage one another day after day, as long as it is still called 'Today,' so that none of you will be hardened by the deceitfulness of sin. For we have become partakers of Christ, if we hold fast the beginning of our assurance firm until the end." To "stay at it, " we must encourage or exhort one another daily. We are prone to wander, that's for sure. So we need people in our lives who will say, "How are you doing today in your walk with the Lord Jesus? Are you cold, hard-hearted, lukewarm? Have you lost your zeal? Are you seeking God in prayer?"

And then it is helpful to take this prayer movement, one day at a time. If you start saying to yourself, "I will never be able to keep this up. I cannot see myself praying like this the rest of my life," then join the club! None of us can see that happening. But if you simply give yourself to Jesus, asking for His Holy Spirit to empower you that day, He will do so. He will meet you in a powerful fashion. "Seek the Lord while He may be found. Call upon Him while He is near. Let the wicked man forsake his ways, and the evil man his thoughts, and let him return to the Lord," (Isaiah 55:6-7).

Finally pray about your praying. Our Korean brethren are legendary for this. They would ask God to help them with their prayer ministries. You need to do the same. To put it another way, pray until you pray. I have noticed that very often, especially when praying by myself, that my mind wanders, that I am having a hard time focusing in the prayer time. But the longer I pray, the more the Spirit meets me, helping to pray more fervently, more faithfully. If you are a long distance runner, like me, then you know that very often the first mile or so of your run is very laborious. You are really struggling, but you know that if you stay at it, the endorphins will kick in soon, and you will run without difficulty. So it is with prayer.

There is nothing more glorious, this side of paradise, than to have the privilege of appearing before God's throne of grace in revival prayer. I challenge you to embrace this privilege and begin a wonderful pilgrimage for the glory of God.

APPENDIX: PRAYER HELPS

Often after conducting a Day of Revival Prayer, I am asked, "This is all sounds very good, but can you be more specific? We have never prayed this way before." I remember a couple attending one of our Days of Revival Prayer and they took home with them a few of these outlines. They said that this was immeasurably helpful to them as they got going on revival prayer. So what follows are a number of outlines on how practically to pray in your church.

HOW TO PRAY IN THE CHURCH

Topics:
How to Spend a Night in Prayer
  Adoration
  Confession
  Thanksgiving
  Supplication
Learning to Pray With a Kingdom Focus
Praying for the Un-gripped
Praying for Your Family
Praying for the Church
Praying for the Nations
What Does it Mean to Pray in the Holy Spirit?
Praying Prevailing Prayer
Revival Prayer
Being Filled With the Spirit
Inductive Bible Study, Kingdom Building in Nehemiah

HOW TO SPEND A NIGHT IN PRAYER

The evening is divided into nine sessions, each one an hour in length and each session is further divided into fifteen minutes of singing and Bible teaching, thirty minutes of prayer, and fifteen minutes of rest and reflection. The prayer sessions will vary from full group to small groups to individuals engaging in prayer. We will pray conversationally, meaning short sentences. Perhaps it is best to use phrases found in each section to assist us in praying intelligently and with substance.

You may rightly ask, why spend a whole night in prayer? The simple answer is that Scripture is replete with examples of the apostles, early church, and Jesus doing it (Luke 6:12, Acts 20:7ff, Luke 22:39ff). It is also interesting to note that such prayer always preceded a momentous occasion in the life of God's people. Jesus chose the twelve disciples after a night of prayer. He went to the cross after a night of prayer. And Paul went to Jerusalem and his eventual arrest after a night of prayer with the church at Troas.

9-10 p.m. Adoration
10-11 p.m. Confession
11-12 a.m. Thanksgiving
12-1 a.m. Supplication- Hallowed be Thy name.
1-2 a.m. Supplication- Thy kingdom come.
2-3 a.m. Supplication- Thy will be done.
3-4 a.m. Supplication- Give us this day our daily bread.
4-5 a.m. Supplication- Forgive us our debts.
5-6 a.m. Supplication- Lead us not into temptation.

SESSION ONE, ADORATION, 9 P.M.

9-9:15, Sing *Immortal, Invisible, God Only Wise*, #38. Teach 1 Chronicles 29:10-20.

9:15-9:45 Full group, conversational prayer.

Read Psalm 145.

We praise you, O God, for your:

Aseity- independence.
Unity- complete in Himself.
Sovereignty- He does as He pleases.
Transcendence- He is beyond time and space.
Holiness- He is without the slightest evil.
Omnipotence- He has all power.
Omnipresence- He is everywhere at once.
Omniscience- He knows all things.
Immensity- He fills up His creation with all His attributes.
Love- it is inexhaustible toward His people.
Immanence- He stoops to our weakness, frailty.
Patience- He is slow to anger.
Grace- He bestows His undeserved favor on His people.
Wisdom- He does all things well, correctly, the first time, every time.

We acknowledge You as:

Elohim- our Creator.
Yahweh- I am who I am, eternal God of the covenant.
Yahweh Jireh- the Lord our provider.
Yahweh Saddiq- the Lord our righteousness.
El Shaddai- the Almighty God.
Yahweh Sabaoath- the Lord of hosts.

9:45-10:00 List and thank God for one thing you learned in this session.

SESSION TWO, CONFESSION, 10 P.M.

10-10:15 Sing *O Thou That Hearest When Sinners Cry*, #485. Teach Psalm 32.

10:15-:10:45 Individuals pray privately, asking and honestly answering the following questions.

Do you have a secret spirit of pride, particularly evident to you after you teach or perform some other Christian service?

Do you have an independent spirit, an unwillingness to accept rebuke from your spouse or an authority figure in your life?

Do you love human praise? One way to know is if you are disappointed when few or none thank you after serving publicly or privately.

Are you given to anger, impatience, being overly sensitive? Do you retaliate in speech addressing others harshly?

Are you stubborn, unteachable, harsh, sarcastic, demanding?

Are you a people pleaser? Do you fear man? Are you afraid to confront a brother or sister in sin? Are you afraid to speak to others about Christ?

Are you jealous of those with more gifts and money than you? Do you secretly devalue those with less than you?

Are you dishonest in business? Do you report all your taxes and do you pay them? Do you deliver your product well and on time? Do you do what you say you will do?

Are you given to unbelief, discouragement, depression, hopelessness?

Are you only formally going through your Christian disciplines?

Are you selfish with your time and money? Do you hoard them? Do you resent intrusions by others on your time?

Are you being faithful to God, obeying Him in the little, big things?

Are you willing to accept rebuke?

Are you exalting yourself, drawing undue attention to yourself? Do you boast about your children?

What are your secret sins, those things you hope the Pastor and Elders never discover?

Are you tithing to your church? Are you holding your possessions loosely?

Is your marriage and family time adequate? Do you make an idol of your family? Do you spend too much time with your family?

Are you developing relationships with non-Christian people?

What are your idols- those people, places, or things which tend to rule your heart and affections?

Are you betraying the confidences of others? Do you gossip, spread rumors, give bad reports?
Is your theology alive, experiential? How do you know?

Are you a racist, bigot? Are you Biblically compassionate toward the poor and suffering of our world?

Do you have a condescending attitude toward brethren with weak theologies?

Do you expect favored status in the church because of your money, position, or power in the world?

Are you filled with the Holy Spirit? Is your life characterized by love, joy, peace, patience, kindness, goodness, gentleness, faithfulness, self-control?

Do you really believe in the sufficiency of Christ and the Bible?

Read and apply 1 John 1:5-10. Do you really believe this?

10:45-11:00 List and thank God for one thing you learned in this session.

SESSION THREE, THANKSGIVING, 11 P.M.

11-11:15 Sing *For The Beauty Of The Earth,* #116. Teach Psalm 139.

11:15-11:30 Individually list 15 temporal blessings, things like food, shelter, clothing. Thank God for them.

11:30-11:45 Break into groups of three or four. These are your groups for the evening. List 15 eternal blessings. See Ephesians 1:3ff,
	Psalm 103:1ff for help. Thank God for them.

11:45-12:00 List and thank God for one thing you learned in this session.

SESSION FOUR, SUPPLICATION- HALLOWED BE THY NAME

12-12:15 Sing *Holy, Holy, Holy*, # 100. Teach Psalm 145.

12:15-12:45 Full group.

As you pray, draw near to God with:
- confidence in His fatherly goodness.
- reverence.
- child-like faith.
- a heart for the glory of God.
- an appropriate understanding of His sovereign power, majesty, gracious condescension.

And acknowledge your inability to honor God as you ought.

And ask God for His grace, that He will enable you and others to acknowledge and highly esteem God and His:
- titles.
- attributes (see Session one).
- ordinances (the preaching of His word, worship, and the sacraments).
- Word (the Bible in your own study and your hearing the word preached. taught).

Ask God to prevent and remove from our community and nation:
- atheism.
- ignorance of God and His ways.
- idolatry (the idols we all tend to worship in our hearts).
- profaneness (all manner of wickedness and perversion in our culture).

Ask God by His overruling providence to direct and carry out all things for His own glory.

12:45-1:00 List and thank God for one thing you learned in this session.

SESSION FIVE, SUPPLICATION- THY KINGDOM COME

1-1:15 Sing *Jesus Shall Reign,* #41. Teach Psalm 66.

1:15-1:45 Small groups.

Acknowledge that all humanity is by nature under the dominion of sin and Satan.

Pray that the kingdom of sin and Satan will be destroyed, that:
-    the gospel will be propagated throughout the world.
-    the Jews will be called, converted in large numbers.
-    the fullness of the Gentile nations will come, every tribe, tongue, people, nation.
-    the church will have the church officers (preachers, elders, deacons, missionaries) she needs to accomplish her task.
-    the church will be purged of her corruption- heresy, lukewarmness, licentiousness.
-    the church will be free, unhindered by the government to carry out her task.
-    the church will purely dispense the ordinances of Christ (preaching, worship, sacraments, discipline).
-    the preaching and teaching of God's word would convert the lost, and comfort and establish the believer.
-    Christ will rule in the hearts of His people, hastening His second coming.
-    God would be pleased to exercise the power of His kingdom in all the world to His own glory.

1:45-2:00 List and thank God for one thing you learned in this session.

SESSION SIX, SUPPLICATION- THY WILL BE DONE

2-2:15 Sing *What 'Er My God Ordains Is Right*, #108. Teach Psalm 34.

2:15-2:45 Individuals. You may wish to walk outside to help you stay awake, as you pray.

In prayer, acknowledge that all humanity is utterly unable and unwilling to know and do God's will, and:
- prone to rebel against His word.
- to murmur against His providence.
- wholly inclined to do the will of the flesh and devil.

Thus pray that God would take from us:
- all blindness, that we would see what we see.
- weakness, lack of faith.
- unwillingness to do or submit to His will.
- perverseness of heart, twisted thinking, affections, and actions.

And ask God to make us willing and able to know, do, and submit to His will with the same:
- humility
- cheerfulness
- faithfulness
- diligence
- zeal
- sincerity
- and consistency as the angels in heaven do.

2:45-3:00 List and thank God for one thing you learned in this session.

SESSION SEVEN, SUPPLICATION- GIVE US THIS DAY OUR DAILY BREAD

3-3:15 Sing *Seek Ye First* and *Though Troubles Assail Us*, #95. Teach Exodus 15.

3:15-3:45 Pray in small groups.

In prayer acknowledge that through Adam's sin and our own sin, we:
- have forfeited the right to all outward blessings in this life.
- deserve to be wholly deprived by God of all outward blessings.
- deserve to have our use of them cursed to us.
- have no reason to believe these sustain or satisfy us.
- do not merit them or by our own hard work procure them.
- are prone to desire, obtain, and use them selfishly, unlawfully.

Thus we pray that we and others, waiting on the providence of God:
- may enjoy a competent portion of outward blessings.
- may have a continued, holy or Biblical, and comfortable use of outward blessings.
- may learn to be content in what outward blessings He gives us.
- may be kept from anything which takes away from our temporal support and comfort.

3:45-4:00 List and thank God for one thing you learned in this session.

SESSION EIGHT, SUPPLICATION- FORGIVE US OUR DEBTS

4-4:15 Sing *Rock of Ages*, #500. Teach Romans 3:23ff.

4:15-4:45 Pray in the full group.

Pray to God, acknowledging that we and all others are guilty of original and actual sin, and are thus, debtors to the justice of God, and that neither we nor any person can make the least satisfaction of that debt. We owe God a debt we cannot pay.

Thus we pray that God:
- of His free grace would,
- through the obedience and satisfaction of Christ,
- received by us and applied by faith,
- acquit, declare us not guilty of both the guilt and punishment our sins deserve,
- accept us in His beloved Son, Jesus,
- that we may continue in His favor and grace to us,
- that He would pardon our daily sins and failings,
- that He would daily fill us with His peace and joy, giving us more and more assurance of His love and forgiveness,
- that we would be emboldened to ask for such, and expect to receive it,
- then, due to all that God has done in forgiving us, we would be able to forgive others who have sinned against us.

Who has wronged you, sinned against you? Who owes you a debt? Are you now able to release them, forgive them of this debt?

4:45-5:00 List and thank God for one thing you learned in this session.

SESSION NINE, SUPPLICATION- LEAD US NOT INTO TEMPTATION

5-5:15 Sing *Rise, My Soul, To Watch And Pray*, #567. Teach I Corinthians 10:1-13.

5:15-5:30 Pray individually, asking God to show you the specific sins with which you are regularly tempted. How well are you fighting against them?

5:30-5:45 Pray in your small groups, using the following:

Pray to God, acknowledging that the most wise, righteous, and gracious God, for varied and holy reasons, may order things in such a way that we are:

- assaulted and for a time led captive by various temptations,
- that Satan, the world, and the flesh may ensnare us,
- and that we, because of our own sinful corruption, weakness, and negligence are:
- subject to being tempted,
- tend to expose ourselves to temptation,
- unable and unwilling to resist them in our own strength or to recover from them, or to learn principles from them,
- worthy to be kept under the power and control of sin and temptation.

We pray that God will so overrule the world, our flesh, and the devil and:
- give and bless to us all His ordinary means of grace (time alone with Him, worship, preaching and teaching, the sacraments),
- and awaken and enliven us to watchfulness and diligence in using these means of grace,
- that we, His people, may be kept from being tempted to sin,
- or if tempted, may be strengthened and enabled to stand in the hour of temptation,
- or if we fall into sin, may be raised from it again and recover from it,
- that our sanctification and eternal salvation may be perfected, improved upon,
- that Satan would be trodden under our feet,
- and we be fully freed from our sin, temptation, and all evil in the glory of heaven.

5:45-6:00 List and thank God for one thing you learned in this session.
Dismissal, Sing *Soldiers Of Christ Arise*, #575

LEARNING TO PRAY WITH A KINGDOM FOCUS

Any church ought to be built on the twin pillars of prayer and evangelism. Admittedly these are the most difficult practices to maintain in the church, but both are essential if a church is to fulfill the Great Commission.

I WHAT DO WE MEAN BY *KINGDOM FOCUSED PRAYER*?

A. Literally and simply it is prayer to the Triune God which focuses on building the rule and reign of Christ in our community and world. Matthew 6:33.
  1. It is earnestly praying the content of the six petitions of the Lord's Prayer, Matthew 6:9-13. See lessons 4-9 of *How To Spend A Night In Prayer* for details on each of these six petitions, or consult the *Larger Catechism* of the *Westminster Confession of Faith,* Questions and Answers 190-196.

B. By *Kingdom Focused Prayer* we do not mean praying:
  1. Organ recitals—Lord, please bless Aunt Matilda's bunion. . .help Uncle Steve to feel better from his cold. . .
  2. Selfishly—Lord help me get a date to the big dance. . .Help me buy a new car, better house, get a better paying job. . .
  3. Temporally—Help my team to win the big game on Saturday. . .Dear Lord help me find a parking space in the next five minutes. . .

C. By *Kingdom Focused Prayer* we do mean praying:
  1. Boldly for Kingdom expansion. See Ephesians 6:19-20.
  2. Expectantly for growth in grace, Colossians 1:9-12.
  3. Humbly for the un-gripped, your family, your family members, church, and world.

D. *Kingdom Focused Prayer* looks like this:
  1. If you, O Lord, get the greatest glory and if I am best sanctified by you healing me from cancer, then please do so, and I will give you sincere, heartfelt thanks.
  2. Gracious and merciful Father, I ask that you would grant my daughter a date to the class dance so that her faith may increase, that she will know that you indeed hear the prayers of your people. . .If you best sanctify me by not allowing me to get that new job, then I fully acquiesce to you in it.

II WHY IS THIS SO IMPORTANT?

A. God is glorified in the salvation of His people.
  1. Psalm 2, 67, 96.
  2. Ephesians 1:4ff.
B. We are learning to think and pray God's thoughts after Him.
  1. Isaiah 61:1ff.
C. We can be sure God answers our kingdom focused prayers.
  1. Matthew 21:22, 1 John 5:13ff.
  2. He most certainly will accomplish His purpose, all His good pleasure, Isaiah 46:9-11, Philippians 1:9-11.

III WHAT DO WE HOPE TO ACCOMPLISH IN *KINGDOM FOCUSED PRAYER?*

A. The Godward dimension—that those for whom we pray will:

1. Seek a greater, experiential knowledge of God.
a) They will know God as their Father, Redeemer, Rock, Fortress, Stronghold, Deliverer.
2. Grow in zeal for the salvation and sanctification of the nations.
a) They will have a love for, burden for the salvation of all the great peoples of the world.
3. Learn to submit joyfully to God in every circumstance.
a) They will overcome the tendency to murmur and complain against things which happen to them in the course of life.

B. The manward dimension—that those for whom we pray will:
1. Make, save, and give away all the money they can for the expansion of the rule and reign of Christ.
a) That they would realize they do not deserve all they have, that it is from God.
2. Forgive those who have wronged them.
a) That they will put away revenge, hostility, bitterness.
3. Stand strong against temptation from the world, flesh, and devil.
a) That they learn to hate and forsake their sin, putting to death the deeds of the body, Romans 8:12, 13, 13:14, Colossians 3:5ff.

Conclusion: Would you say that your prayers have been Kingdom Focused in the past? How? How not? If not, what specific steps can you now take to make them more kingdom focused?

PRAYING FOR THE UN-GRIPPED

The degree of one's love for people can -be measured in his prayer for their salvation. Do you have ungripped people on your heart and are you praying that they will come to know the love of God in Christ Jesus our Lord?

I WHAT DO WE MEAN BY UN-GRIPPED?
A. In today's world the term Christian has lost a great deal of its meaning.
  1. To many the term Christian means:
  a) An American. . .church-goer. . .political conservative. . .
  2. Many whom we know are church-goers and they profess to be Christians.
  a) Others are adherents to other religions and hence believe all is well with every person's soul and standing with God.

B. By *un-gripped* we mean:
  1. Those who may claim to be Christians, who are church-goers, or who follow some religion, but who give no indication that they see their sin, who have not experienced the grace of God, who do not see the necessity of Christ's cross and atoning death, who see no need for repentance of sin and faith in Jesus Christ, who fail to glory in the cross of Christ, who fail to see Christ's death and resurrection as their greatest joy and need.
  2. Those who seldom, if ever, speak of Christ's passion (suffering), death, resurrection, those who fail to see this as vital to their existence now and for eternity.

C. A person gripped with the gospel cannot stop speaking what he has seen and heard, Acts 4:20. Peter is told by the Sanhedrin to stop preaching Jesus and he says that he cannot stop speaking what he has seen and heard about Jesus. He is gripped with the gospel.
  1. This affects one's speech, life, actions, and attitudes.

II HOW DO WE PRAY FOR THE UN-GRIPPED?
A. Pray, asking the Holy Spirit to make known to the person the seven I Am statements Jesus makes in the gospel of John.
  1. I am the bread of life, John 6:35. . .I am the light of the world, John 8:12. . .I am the door of the sheep, John 10:7. . .I am the door, John 10:9. . .I am the resurrection and the life, John 11:25. . .I am the way, the truth, and the life, John 14:6. . .I am the vine, John 15:5.
  2. We can pray—Father, for my friend who is hungry for meaning in life, would you reveal by your Holy Spirit Jesus to be the bread of life, the One who alone can sustain his hunger. . .Gracious God, for my friend who is living in darkness, would you reveal by your Spirit Jesus to be the light of the world. . .Merciful Lord, for my friend who has lost his way, who is believing the lies of the world and devil, would you by your Spirit reveal Jesus as the way and the truth. . .

B. Make a list of:
  1. Family members. . .work associates. . .neighbors. . .who are ungripped. List them   below:

_____

_____

2. Then pray. . .pray. . .pray. . .believe God will convert them.

III WHAT RESULTS FROM PRAYING FOR THE UN-GRIPPED?
A. Some are regenerated (born again) and converted, turning from their sin and believing on the Lord Jesus Christ, Mark 1:15, Ezekiel 37:1ff.
1. Consider the wonderful promises, Daniel 12:2-3.
a) They become a savor of life unto life, 2 Corinthians 2:16.

B. Some remain dead in their sins and are on the road to destruction.
1. Matthew 7:13-14, Ephesians 2:1-3, 4:18ff, 2 Corinthians 2:14-16, Hebrews 12:24ff.

Assignment: Make a list of un-gripped friends, etc., using the list above and begin praying specifically for their salvation, using the *I am* statements of Jesus as a model.

PRAYING FOR YOUR FAMILY

We want to learn to pray with a kingdom focus in all areas of life, including our own family. Our tendency may be to pray for:

- our children's popularity or athletic success.
-our daughter to marry a well-educated, prosperous young man.
-our son to marry a beautiful young lady.
-our children to be spared hardship and trial in life.

These however are fleeting and shallow requests which lack the eternal and sanctifying nature of true God controlled living.

I HOW THEN SHOULD WE PRAY FOR OUR FAMILY WITH A KINGDOM FOCUS?

A. Keep in mind that prayer according to God's word, if other conditions are met, is insured of His favor, that He will in fact answer it. See 1 John 5:14ff.

B. So we should pray scripture, which addresses godly character, back to God. Since such is according to God's will, we ought to expect the answer from Him.

C. Pray:
- Matthew 5:3ff the beatitudes.
- Romans 5:1ff.
- 2 Peter 1:4ff.
- Proverbs. .consider praying one chapter of proverbs each day—for your children and others. "Do not speak in the hearing of a fool, for he will despise the wisdom of your words, Proverbs 23:9. You could pray, "Father I ask that you so work in the hearts and minds of my children that they give strong evidence of Biblical wisdom. I ask that you not allow them to fall into folly, that they give no evidence of being what the Bible calls a fool."
- wife, pray for your husband to love you as Christ loved the church and gave Himself up for her, that he will be a loving and cherishing provider for his family.
- husband, pray for your wife to submit humbly to your loving, covenantal leadership, that she will be a Biblical helper to you in your role to lead your family.

II WHY SHOULD WE PRAY FOR OUR FAMILY, USING A KINGDOM FOCUS?
A. It restricts-
1. Shallowness. . .temporalness. .
Illus: Esau in Genesis 25:27ff.
B. It enhances.
1. One's holiness. .living with heaven in full view.
Illus: Proverbs 3-4.

III HOW TO CONDUCT FAMILY WORSHIP.

We recommend Terry Johnson's book Leading in *Family Worship* as an excellent and practical guide.

Having said this, keep in mind:
-    the Father's responsibility as covenant head. See Ephesians 5:23, 6:4, Proverbs 4-5.
-    the battle for consistency.

- The tendency to forget variety. .to drift toward dead formalism. .to neglect gearing the time toward the age of your children.

Conclusion: If you are a husband, are you meeting regularly with your children and wife? If you do not have a plan, why not get one right now? Begin to pray for your spouse and children with these things in mind.

PRAYING FOR THE CHURCH

You probably know from experience that most prayer meetings turn into organ recitals ("Lord, please help Jim overcome his cold.") We are not saying God is not interested in our health or other temporal issues, for surely He is. However we are saying He wants to do far more than simply heal people of disease. How then are we to pray for the people in our church?

I WHAT DO WE MEAN BY PRAYING FOR OUR CHURCH WITH A KINGDOM FOCUS?

A. We do not simply mean praying for:
- physical woes. .numerical growth. .the church budget to be met. .bigger programs.

B. We do mean prayer which focuses on building Christ's kingdom in the church.
1. Individual growth in grace, Romans 5:1-5.

2. Familial growth in grace, Ephesians 5:22, 25, 6:1-4.

3. Congregational growth in grace, Romans 12:1-2.

II WHY PRAY FOR KINGDOM GROWTH IN THE CHURCH?

A. It glorifies God, 1 Cor.10:31.

B. It edifies believers, Ephesians 1:18ff.

C. It testifies to unbelievers, Matthew 5:14.

III HOW ARE WE TO PRAY FOR KINGDOM GROWTH IN THE CHURCH?

A. Use prayers in Scripture as a model for your own prayers.
1. Ephesians 1:18-19, Ephesians 3:13-20, Philippians 1:9-11, Colossians 1:9-12. For example, using Colossians 1:9-12, you may wish to paraphrase and pray, "Father, indeed you are merciful and slow to anger, abounding in loving kindness and truth. Therefore I ask that you grant our the people of our church grace to walk in a manner worthy of the Lord, to bring forth fruit in every good work, to please God in every respect, to increase in the knowledge of God, to persevere in difficult circumstances, to forbear with difficult people, to always be giving thanks to the Father who has qualified us to share the inheritance with the saints in light."

B. Ask God to build in your fellow believers the qualities found in Matthew 5:33ff (the beatitudes), Romans 5:3ff, Galatians 5:22-23, 2 Peter 1:5ff.

C. Ask God to build in fellow believers obedience to the commands found in: Romans 6:12-13, Romans 8:13, Ephesians 4-6, Colossians 3.

D. Ask God to build in fellow believers greater trust in the truths based on: Romans 8, 1 Corinthians 13, 2 Corinthians 4:14-18.

E. Ask God to build in fellow believers greater awareness of heaven from: 1 Corinthians 15:51-58, Revelation 1,4-5,19-21.

F. Ask God to build in fellow believers greater trust in the ministry of the Holy Spirit, to:

– not grieve the Spirit, Ephesians 5:30. This is like hurting deeply one whom you love.

-   not quench the Spirit, 1 Thessalonians 5:19. This is like pouring water on a campfire. When the Holy Spirit moves you to pray for someone, and you choose not to do it, then you are quenching the Spirit.

-   not resist the Spirit, Acts 7:51. Like when the Spirit convicts you of a particular sin and you refuse to repent of it.

-   to be filled with the Spirit, Ephesians 5:18. Like one who is drunk with wine (his speech, walk, thinking are all effected by the alcohol), so one filled with the Holy Spirit finds his speech, way of living, and his thinking all positively effected, acting more like Jesus.

We pray this way so that we may be bold in faith, life, and witness, Acts 4:31.

IV HOW AND WHY SHOULD WE PRAY FOR OUR CHURCH OFFICERS?

A. Satan preys on church leaders. See Luke 22:31ff.
1. He knows that to bring down into grievous sin a pastor, elder, or deacon greatly hinders the work of Christ's kingdom. It lends credence to the notion that Christianity is filled with hypocrites.
2. **But Jesus promises to pray for us and He wants us to intercede as well for our** church leaders. Luke 22:32, Hebrews 7:25. Paul asks for prayer, Ephesians 6:18-19, Colossians 4:3.

B. How should we pray for church officers?
1. Perhaps a good way to remember to pray for them is to pray at every meal for your pastor as well as one elder and deacon.

C. And for what should you pray?
1. For them to be devoted to prayer, Colossians 4:2.
2. For them to be focused on the Great Commission, Matthew 28:18-20, Acts 1:8.
3. For them to shepherd the flock of God faithfully, 1 Peter 5:1-4.
4. For them to grow in Biblical holiness, humility, love, and faithfulness, 1 Corinthians 13:4ff, Galatians 5:22-23.
5. For your pastor to preach and teach the word of God accurately, boldly, faithfully, 2 Timothy 2:15ff, 4:1-5.

Conclusion: How is your present prayer life? Are you praying for your church with a kingdom focus? Are you praying through Scripture? How do you think you may quench or grieve the Holy Spirit?

PRAYING FOR THE NATIONS

While certainly we ought to pray for the un-gripped, our family, and our church God also calls us to pray for the world, that the gospel will be propagated all over the world so that every people group may hear the good news of Jesus Christ in their own language and in their own cultural context. May God so work in us that we become world Christians. Not worldly Christians but those who have a heart for spreading the gospel to all the world, those who take an interest in salvation of all the great peoples of the world.

I WHAT DO WE MEAN BY PRAYING FOR THE NATIONS?
A. By this we do not mean:
1. Political activism.
2. Merely reading about other cultures.
3. Merely visiting other cultures.

B. By this we do mean:
1. Developing a heart for world evangelization.
2. Asking God to put on your heart particular nations, people groups, missionaries, indigenous workers for whom you can pray.

C. Consider Biblical evidence calling us to gain God's heart for all the nations.
1. Genesis 12:1-3, Psalm 59:13, Psalm 96, Isaiah 2:2-4, Isaiah 52:7ff, Matthew 28:18-20, Acts 1:8, Revelation 5:9-10.

II WHY ARE WE TO PRAY FOR THE NATIONS?
A. Since God ordains the ends (the salvation of His people), He also ordains the means to the end (prayer and evangelism).
1. Ephesians 1:3-4, Romans 9:1ff, Romans 10:13-17.
2. Because man is dead in his sins, he cannot and will not believe unless the Holy Spirit draws him and regenerates him and this comes only through the prayers of God's people. See Romans 8:26-27.

III HOW ARE WE TO PRAY FOR THE NATIONS?
A. Pray for the Holy Spirit to open doors for the gospel in hostile, unevangelized regions.

B. Ephesians 6:18ff. Especially among the Japanese Shintoists. .Hindus. . Buddhists. .Muslims. .animists in South America and Africa.

C. Pray for the Holy Spirit to promote unity, humility, and trust between missionary team members, organizations, and national workers. John 17:18-26.

D. Pray for the Holy Spirit to strengthen His suffering and persecuted people and for Him to expand His church in the midst of that persecution. Matthew 5:10-12, Colossians 1:11.

E. Pray for the Holy Spirit to bring conversion to the lost and to establish churches in areas where the church is weak or non-existent.

Assignment: Pick out two or three missionaries you know or feel especially close to, and begin praying daily for them as noted above.

WHAT DOES IT MEAN TO PRAY IN THE HOLY SPIRIT?

1 Corinthians 14:15, ". . .I shall pray with the spirit and I shall pray with the mind also; I shall sing with the spirit and I shall sing with the mind also."

John Bunyan defines praying in the Holy Spirit as:

The sincere, sensible, affectionate pouring out of the heart or soul to God, through Christ, in strength and assistance of the Holy Spirit, for such things as God promised, or according to His word, for the good of the church, with submission in faith to the will of God.

- a sincere pouring out of the soul to God, Psalm 66:17-18, 16:1-4, Jeremiah 29:12-13.

- a sensible or intelligent, Biblically well-informed pouring out of the soul to God. . an awareness of need for mercy because of our sin, Psalm 38:8-10. .an awareness of mercy received which yields comfort, strength, encouragement, Psalm 103:1-4. .an awareness of mercy to be received in the future, Genesis 32:10-11, Daniel 9:3-4.

- an affectionate, opening of the heart or soul to God, perhaps even in groans, weeping, sighs, Psalm 38:9, 42:2-4, Deuteronomy 4:29.

- through Christ. Christ is our mediator, the One who makes access to the Father possible, Daniel 9:17, Psalm 25:11, John 14:6.

- by the strength and help or assistance of the Holy Spirit. Only such petitions can be according to the will of God, Romans 8:26-27, Matthew 21:22.
- for such things God has promised us in His word, Psalm 119:25-28, Daniel 9:2-3, 1 John 5:14-15.

- for the good of the church, the glory of God. .advancement of Christ's kingdom. .benefit of God's people. .John 17, Jesus' High Priestly prayer.

- in submission to the will of God, Matthew 6:10, 1 Corinthians 2:11. The Larger *Catechism of the Westminster Confession of Faith* says that we are to learn to submit to God's will in everything with humility, cheerfulness, faithfulness, diligence, zeal, sincerity, and consistency.

To pray in the Holy Spirit means:
- He gives us the words to pray, Colossians 3:16.

- He gives us earnestness in prayer, Romans 8:26-27.

- He takes our prayer to the Father who acts on our behalf, Numbers 14:11-21. Israel sins. .Moses intercedes. .God answers, choosing not to destroy His people.

Conclusion: How does "praying in the Spirit" differ from most praying we hear in Reformed churches today? How will praying in the Spirit affect the way you pray?

PRAYING PREVAILING PRAYER, James 5:16

Introduction: Surely the low state of Christianity in the U.S. ought to move us to learn to pray prevailing prayer. What is it? How do we engage in it?

I WHAT IS PREVAILING PRAYER? - it is not merely having a desire to pray or actually to engage in the activity of prayer.
- it is prayer that works, that God answers, James 4:2,3.
- it is prayer for specific, kingdom focused requests, Mt.6:9ff.
- it is prayer according to God's revealed will in His word, 1 John 5:14-15.
- it is prayer that submits to the will of God, 2 Samuel 12:15-23.
- it is prayer that is earnest because the need is so great, Gen.32:26.
- it is prayer offered with the right motives- the glory of God and the good of mankind, Ps.119:53, 136.
- it is prayer born of and bathed in the Holy Spirit, Rom.8:26-27.
- it is prayer which perseveres, is consistent, never gives up, Luke 22:44.
- it is prayer where one stays at it, praying often, Luke 11:5ff.
- it is prayer offered in the name of Jesus, standing on all He is, has done, is doing, and will do, John 14:14.
- it is prayer where one denounces, hates, turns from his many sins, Is.59:2.
- it is prayer offered in faith, Mt.21:22.
Application: List three characteristics of prayer most deficient in your own quest for prevailing prayer.
Application: List three specific requests for which you will purpose to pray prevailingly.

II HOW DO WE ENGAGE IN PREVAILING PRAYER?
A. God must break up the fallow ground of our hearts, Hos.10:12.
- to ransack our hearts in order to reveal our sin, Ps.139:23-24.
- to drive us to grief, confession, repentance, restitution, Joel 2:13.

B. How do we do this?
1. See and feel our sins of commission. These are:
- loving, desiring the world and its comforts more than God or Jesus.
- living with pride, thinking we are better than others, being harsh or judgmental, racist or bigoted.
- being envious, jealous of someone and his possessions, accomplishments.
- speaking harshly, judgmentally of other believers.
- receiving, believing, passing on what you've heard about another when you are not in a position to do anything about it.
- lying by misrepresenting, hiding, or shading the truth in any circumstance..
- cheating others like your employer, clients by over charging or under working.
- living hypocritically, giving fellow Christians the impression you are more godly than you really are.
- robbing God by not tithing
- robbing the government by not paying all your taxes. .taking more benefits than you are justly due.
- robbing your spouse and children by spending money and time foolishly.
- sinful anger in your speech and actions with anyone.
- overlording your wife, children, subordinates with harsh, cruel, micro- managing.
Application: List three major sins of commission. . how do you need to repent?
2.See and feel our sins of omission.
- ingratitude to God for all He is, has done.

- lack of love for all God is, has done for you and yours.
- lack of hunger for, study of God's word.
- lack of faith or trust in the promises of God and His word.
- failure to pursue the means of grace personally, familially, and personally.
- pursuing worship casually, with lukewarmness.
- lack of burden for the lost in your family, neighborhood, nation.
- lack of guarding your heart against idolatry, whoring after false gods.
- lack of concern, spiritual maturity, welfare of other Christians.
- failure to practice Biblical self-denial.
Application: List three sins of omission. . .How do you need to repent?

III HOW DO WE PRAY IN FAITH? Mark 11:24
A. We are broadly to believe two things.
1. That God is . . .He rewards those who diligently seek His face, Heb.11:6.
2. That we will receive.
Illus: Countless examples from the Dani tribe of Irian Jaya. .

B.   *We specifically are to know and plead the promises of God.*
- Is.59:19
- Is.65:24
- Ps.103:17-18
- Is.43:1-3
- Deut.4:29
- 1 Kings 8:33

C. We confidently are to believe we will receive.
- Mt.7:7-11.
- Heb.5:7
- John 11:42
- 2 Cor.12:7-9.
Application: Where are you falling short? Pick three promises. .plead them before the throne of grace.

Chapter 14

Questions of observation.
What is happening in:
- verse 1, When is this happening?
- verses 2-8, Why are we told all these details? Why is this important?
- verses 9-10.

What do verses 3 -5 mean. .What parallels exist today in the covenant community?
What reason does Asa give for Judah's prosperity and peace, v.7? How would you apply this to us today?
What is the difference in troop strength between Judah and Ethiopia? What parallels can you think of today?

What is the context of Asa's prayer in v. 11? List three or four key points from this prayer which ought to compose our prayer as well.

How did God respond to Asa's prayer, v.12-15? What parallels can we make for today?

List three take-aways from this passage concerning prayer with a kingdom focus.

Let's pray these now.

Chapter 15

When are these reforms taking place, vs.10?

Five years between chapters 14 and 15. What does this tell us about spiritual declension?

Why do you think spiritual declension occurs?

What are the necessary conditions for spiritual renewal and revival? See v. 2, 4.

What happens to families, churches, nations which move toward spiritual declension? See v. 5-6.

How did Asa respond to Azariah's exhortation? v. 8-14.
What does vs. 12 mean, "they entered into a covenant to seek the Lord God of their fathers with all their heart and soul?"

Verse 13, Is this harsh? Why or why not? See Ex.22:20, Deut. 13:6-11.

Verse 14, How would we make an oath to God today?
Verse 15, What does this verse mean. . ."sworn with their whole heart. . .sought Him earnestly, and He let them find Him." What does this look like today?

Verse 16, What are the horrid images people worship today? What are we to do about them? How?

Verse 17, What does "high places removed" mean? How can we apply this today? How could Asa's heart be blameless all his days with high places still existing?
Verse 19, Another twenty years of peace and prosperity came. Why? How do we find peace today in families, churches, nations?
List three take-aways from this chapter on kingdom focused prayer.

Now, let's pray them.

Chapter 16

Verse 1, What is happening?

Verses 2-3, What is wrong with this picture?

Verses 4-5, Seemingly one could say, "So far, so good" as far as Judah is concerned. . .What tells you that this does not bode well for Judah? What are examples of all appearing well in today's world?

Verse 6, Why is financial prosperity a notoriously false indicator of one's spiritual health? How do people today buy into this?

Verse 7, The prophet Hanani confronts Asa. . . What does he say? How does this apply today? What happened to him, v. 10? What evidence do you have that preachers can be man-pleasers? How is this evident?

Verse 8, How is Hanani appealing to church history? How can we apply this today?

Verse 9, What does this mean? See Proverbs 15:3, Zechariah 4:10. What are the signs that one's heart is completely God's? Why does trusting the creature rather than the Creator lead to "wars"?

Verse 10, How could Asa fall to such depths? What is the warning for us?

Verses 11-14, How did Asa finish? What steps can we take to insure that we finish the race well?

List three take-aways from this chapter, moving us toward kingdom focused prayer?

Now let's pray them.

BEING FILLED WITH THE SPIRIT

Introduction: If Romans 3:10ff is true. .if Romans 5:6 is true. .if 250 years of Unitarianism has cast a cloud of unbelief over new england. .then are we not desperate for the Spirit's fullness, presence, and power?

I THE COMMAND.
A. *Positively stated, Eph.5:18. .Luke 11:9-13.*

B. *Negatively stated, Eph.4:30. .I Thess.5:19. .Acts 7:51. .*
Illus: "Be like Mike. ."

II OUR FAILURE AND WHY.
A. *Dominated, controlled by the Holy Spirit is seldom our consistent experience.*

B. *Look at Galatians 5:19ff, which rather* consistently defines your behavior?

C. *Why do we fail?*
1. Are you living in hypocrisy?
2. Are you living with inordinate frivolity, carelessness?
3. Are you living with pride, being convinced of your own superiority?
4. Are you worldly minded, thinking primarily of acquiring wealth, ease?
5. Are you seldom confessing, forsaking your sins of commission, omission?
6. Are you neglecting a specific biblical duty, like tithing, corporate, family, or individual worship? Loving your wife? Discipling your children?
7. Are you resisting the Spirit? When convicted of sin through preaching or a rebuke by your wife or a friend, are you defensive? Do you explain it away? Do you give mere lip service?
8. Are you without the Spirit's power? If so, then it is because you do not want it. Are you willing to do what is necessary to be filled with the Spirit?
9. Are you asking the Father for the Holy Spirit? Do you earnestly seek God for Him?

III RESULTS FROM BEING FILLED WITH THE SPIRIT. *You will have:*
A. *An increased heavenly mindedness, Col.3:1ff.*
1. The opposite is worldly mindedness, Phil.3:18-19.
a) A way of life, "walk"
b) Enemies of Christ. .how? Deny necessity, power of cross. .
c) Their end is destruction. .
d) Sensual desires—delight in shameful things. .think/live temporally, materially

B. *An increased distress over the condition of the church, Rev.2-3.*
1. Ephesus—loss of our first love. .
2. Smyrna—apparent tendency to fear persecution, martyrdom. .
3. Pergamum—taking money at expense of God's kingdom, people. . antinomianism. .
4. Thyatira—tolerating false teaching. .
5. Sardis—casualness, lack of zeal for God's glory. .
6. Philadelphia—apparent tendency to not persevere to the end, to grow faint hearted. .
7. Laodicea—pride, uselessness in God's kingdom. .

C. *An increased distress over the state of the gospel ministry, 2 Tim.4:1ff*
1. Poor state of gospel preaching, 1-2.
2. Lack of desire to hear, obey, act upon gospel preaching, 3-4.

3. Failure of ministers to follow the Apostolic example, 5-8.

D. An increased opposition from:
1. Church—liberalism. .lukewarmness. .professionalism. .
2. World—universalism. .political correctness. .principled pluralism. .
3. Flesh—recurring sins. .discouragement. .fear of man. .
4. Devil—temptation to quit. .embrace grievous sin. .

E. An increased peace with God.
1. Jesus is praying, Rom.8:34, Heb.7:25.
2. The Holy Spirit is praying, Rom.8:26-27.
3. The angels ministry to you, Heb.1:13-14.

F. An increased peace of conscience, 2 Peter 1:2-4. The Spirit:
1. Will teach you.
2. Prompt you.
3. Empower you.
4. Embolden you.
5. Use you to build up believers.
6. Use you to convert the lost.
7. Strengthen you in affliction.
8. Prepare you for death.
9. Will overcome impatience, irritability, mean spiritedness.
Conclusion: May we therefore earnestly seek for the filling of the Holy Spirit.

INDUCTIVE BIBLE STUDY, KINGDOM BUILDING IN NEHEMIAH

Chapter 1, A Model Kingdom Prayer

v. 1-2, what is the historical setting?

v. 3, what is the report?

v. 4, what is Nehemiah's response? What does he do? Describe his *pathos* or emotion.

Does our present condition in the U. S. parallel the report Nehemiah hears? If so, then how?

Have you ever responded in like manner to such a report on the condition of Christ's kingdom? How? If not, why not?

Consider details of Nehemiah's prayer, v. 5-11.

v. 5, what does he tell God about who He is? Why does He use this language?

v. 6, what does he ask? Why does he ask it?

v. 7, what does he pray? Why does he tie the commandments to Moses?

v. 8, 9, notice the legal, covenantal language. What happens to those unfaithful to God's covenant? What happens to those who repent of their unfaithfulness? What does God promise?

v. 10, note the covenantal language. What is Nehemiah affirming?

v. 11, what does Nehemiah ask of the Lord? In this context, how would you define success?
Look again at v. 5, how should we begin intercessory prayer for the kingdom? Why is corporate and personal confession of sin so vital in prayer for the kingdom?

How do promised kingdom curses and blessings affect us in prayer for the kingdom?

What would *success* look like in your church?
Let's pray these truths back to God.
Chapter 2, Preparation for Model Kingdom Living

v. 1-2, Nehemiah could not hide his sadness. Why not? How does this apply to us?

v. 3, how did Nehemiah obtain such boldness to speak directly to the king? How may we get such boldness?

v. 4, Nehemiah has favor with the king. What is the reason for it?

v. 5, Note the specific objective. What is it? What is your church's purpose and vision?

v. 6-8, what does this tell you about Nehemiah's planning? Why did the king grant Nehemiah's request? What should precede planning?

v. 10, why are Sanballat and Tobiah displeased? Do you think Nehemiah was anticipating opposition? What opposition should we expect? From who?

v. 11, 12-16, what is happening here? Why at night? Why a few men? Why did he not reveal his plan? Why no other animals with him? Ought everyone be privy to a leader's plans? If not, why not? If so, when and why?

v. 13-15, why is so much detail given in Nehemiah's report?
17a, note Nehemiah's honest, blunt assessment. Why must a leader gain all the facts about the current situation?

v. 17b, note Nehemiah's direct exhortation and reason. Why is it vital that church members know your church's purpose and vision? Do you think your people know it? Own it? Why or why not?

Why is it difficult to move people to a common purpose and vision?

v. 18, how do the people respond? Why do they agree? How can you better get people on board with your purpose and vision?

v. 19, how did outsiders respond? How might the devil, unbelievers mock your church?

v. 20, how does Nehemiah respond? What does this say about how we ought to respond to mocking, apathy by the enemies of Christ's kingdom?

How does repairing the ruins of the wall in Jerusalem parallel repairing the ruins of our once Christian culture?
Let's pray these truths back to God?

Chapter 3, Unanimity in Repairing the Ruins

Note the detail given by the author, beginning with work at the Sheep gate and moving counterclockwise until he reaches the Sheep gate again.

Why do you think the author goes into such detail of describing which people were to build which section of the wall?

Do you think that only the "little people" are engaged in this work? Why or why not?

What does this tell you about the work or rebuilding the ruins in your community?

Why are all your people, not just the elders, staff, and ministry team leaders important? How can you better communicate their importance in this work?

Look at verse 5. Are all the people "on board" with Nehemiah's effort? What does this say about repairing the ruins through your church in your part of the world? Must you wait for all to be "on board"? Why or why not? What should be your attitude toward those slow to get "on board", or who refuse to do so altogether?

Why is unity in the work of repairing the ruins so vital?

What does unity look like? Where does honest disagreement come in? How should you handle disunity, disagreement?

Let's pray what we have learned back to God.

Chapter 4, Handling Outside Opposition in Repairing the Ruins

A little background concerning Sanballat and Tobiah may be helpful here. Sanballat is a Babylonian name which means "*the moon god gives life.*" Sanballat and his descendants had governed Samaria for over 100 years. He may have worshiped Yahweh in some syncretistic form (as the Samaritans were known to do, 2 Kings 17:24ff).

Tobiah was probably the governor of Ammon, east of Judah, and his name means *the Lord is good.* He may have worshipped Yahweh too, though in a syncretistic way. See Nehemiah 6:17-18, 13:4.

Look at verses 1-3, What is happening?

Why do you think Sanballat and Tobiah are opposing the people of God? See Nehemiah 2:10.

How are they opposing them?

Note verses 4-5, What does Nehemiah do about this opposition?

How should we apply this in our day? What do we do with the so-called imprecatory Psalms? See Psalm 5, 139:19-22.

Note verse 6, How did this opposition affect Nehemiah and the workers? How should you apply this to outside opposition you may face? What type of outside opposition can you expect in your great work of rebuilding the ruins of God's kingdom in your community?

Note verses 7-8. Did the opposition go away? It seems to have broadened to include more enemies of God's kingdom. How did this opposition escalate? What form did it take?

Note verse 9, How did Nehemiah respond to this escalation of opposition? What does this mean for us?

Note verses 10-12, What is the gist of the bad news Judah brings to Nehemiah?

See verses 13-14, What does Nehemiah do with the bad news Judah brings? What does this tell you about godly leadership?

Look at verses 15-18, How does Nehemiah exhibit practical faith? How should this play out in your great work of rebuilding the ruins?

Look at verses 19-20, how does Nehemiah maintain vision for the fainthearted? How can you do the same?

Note verses 21-23, What is Nehemiah telling us? What does this tell us about vigilance? How can we maintain vigilance in a culture given to peace and affluence?

Pray what you have learned back to God.
Chapter 5, Handling Inside Opposition in Rebuilding the Ruins

Note verses 1-5, What is happening here? See Exodus 22:22-27, Leviticus 25:35-38.

Look at verses 6-8, How does Nehemiah respond to this report? What does he do and why? What does this tell you about godly leadership?

Note verses 9-11, What is the primary motivation for repentance and obedience? What does Nehemiah call them to do? Why is refraining from usury not enough? How does he expect them to go forward in interacting with the poor in the covenant community?

Note verses 12-13, How do the people respond? How does Nehemiah put "teeth" in their promise? What is the symbolism he uses in verse 13? Did the people "get it". How do you know? What does this mean for you concerning the poor in your city?

Note verses 14-16, How was Nehemiah's behavior different from previous rulers? Why was his behavior different? In verse 16, why do you think he refused to buy land? What does this say about gaining wealth? Is it sinful? When and when not?

Note verses 17-18, Nehemiah is obviously quite wealthy and, due to his position as governor, must entertain powerful people. Does he exact taxes due him from the people to entertain the powerful? Why not? What does this tell you about Nehemiah's leadership role and sensitivity to the "little people"?

Why does he pray this in verse 19? How do we apply this to our living in this world of both plenty and want?
Pray what you have learned back to God.

Chapter 6, Moving Forward In The Face Of Opposition

Verses 1-2, What do Sanballat and the others want from Nehemiah? How do we know that Nehemiah is "on" to them?

Verse 3, How does Nehemiah respond? What does this say about Nehemiah's ability to focus on a great work when others seek to distract him from it?

What are your great enemies in your effort to rebuild the ruins of your community?

Verses 4,-5, Note their persistence. How do your enemies persist in their efforts to dissuade you from your great work?
Verses 6-7, What is the purpose of Sanballat's letter?

Verse 8, How does Nehemiah refute the letter?

What is the best defense against potentially damaging accusations?

Verse 9, How does Nehemiah ultimately look for a remedy?

How should you apply this to your present ministry?

Verses 10-14, Note the relentless opposition, now seen in Shemaiah. What is happening here? How do you think Nehemiah "saw through" their deception?

What does this say about your need to be vigilant in spiritual warfare?

Verses 15-16, What happens to opposition when God does a mighty work?

Verses 17-19. Deception can persist. Should you expect great opposition to go away completely? Permanently? When will opposition end?

How are we to live in the meantime?

List two things you learned from this discussion. Now pray them back to God for the sake of His kingdom in your community.

BIBLIOGRAPHY

Allen, Roland. *The Spontaneous Expansion Of The Church And The Causes Which Hinder It.*. [1st American ed. Grand Rapids: W.B. Eerdmans Pub. Co., 1962.

Baker, Allen M.. *Seeking A Revival Culture: Essays On Fortifying An Anemic Church*. Eugene, Or.: Resource Publications, 2009.

Bennett, William W.. *A Narrative Of The Great Revival Which Prevailed In The Southern Armies During The Late Civil War Between The States Of The Federal Union*. 1877. Reprint, Philadelphia: Claxton, Remsen & Haffelfinger, 1877.

Blair, William Newton, and Bruce F. Hunt. *The Korean Pentecost And The Sufferings Which Followed*. Edinburgh: Banner of Truth Trust, 1977.

Boice, James Montgomery. *Acts: An Expositional Commentary*. Pbk. ed. Grand Rapids, Mich.: Baker Books, 2006.

Bonhoeffer, Dietrich, and John W. Doberstein. *Life Together*. Ristampa. ed. San Francisco: HarperSanFrancisco, 1993.

Brook, B.. *The Lives Of The Puritans: Containing A Biographical Account Of Those Divines Who Distinguished Themselves In The Cause Of Religious Liberty, From The Reformation Under Queen Elizabeth, To The Act Of Uniformity In 1662*. Pittsburgh: Soli Deo Gloria Publications, 19961994.

Brook, Benjamin. *The Lives Of The Puritans, Vol 3*. S.l.: Soli Deo Gloria, 1994.

Chilton, David. *The Days of Vengeance*. Fort Worth: Dominion Press, 1987.

Couper, W. J., and Richard Owen Roberts. *Scotland Saw His Glory: A History Of Revivals In Scotland*. Wheaton, Ill.: International Awakening Press, 1995.

DeMar, Gary. *Last Days Madness: Obsession Of The Modern Church*. 4th ed. Atlanta, Ga.: American Vision, 1999.

Dekker, John, and Lois Neely. *Torches Of Joy: The Dynamic Story Of A Stone Age Tribe's Encounter With The Gospel Of Jesus Christ*. 3rd ed. Seattle: YWAM, 1999.

Edwards, Brian. *Can We Pray For Revival*. Faverdale North Darlington, England: Evangelical Press, 2004.

Edwards, Jonathan. *The Life of David Brainerd, Chiefly Extracted From His Diary*. Grand Rapids, Mich.: Baker Book House, 1981.

Evans, Eifion. *The Welsh Revival Of 1904*. 3rd ed. Bridgend, Wales: Bryntirion Press, 1987.

Fawcett, Arthur. *The Cambuslang Revival; The Scottish Evangelical Revival Of The Eighteenth Century.*. London: Banner of Truth Trust, 1971.

Gentry, Kenneth L.. *He Shall Have Dominion: A Postmillennial Eschatology*. Tyler, Tex.: Institute for Christian Economics, 1992.

Hulse, Erroll. *Give Him No Rest: A Call To Prayer For Revival*. Darlington (England): Evangelical Press, 1991.

Jones, David Martyn. *Revival*. Westchester, Ill.: Crossway Books, 1987.

Jones, J. Morgan, William Morgan, and John Aaron. *The Calvinistic Methodist Fathers Of Wales*. Edinburgh: Banner of Truth Trust, 2008.

Kelly, Douglas F.. *Preachers With Power: Four Stalwarts Of The South*. Edinburgh: Banner of Truth Trust, 1992.

"LECRAE - BEAUTIFUL FEET LYRICS." Lyrics. http://www.songlyrics.com/lecrae/beautiful-feet-lyrics/ (accessed January 26, 2013).

Lloyd-Jones, Martyn. *Revival*. Westchester, Ill.: Crossway Books, 1987.

Mathison, Keith A.. *Postmillennialism: An Eschatology Of Hope*. Phillipsburg, N.J.: P&R Pub., 1999.

Murray, Iain Hamish. *David Martyn Lloyd-Jones: The First Forty Years, 1899-1939*. Edinburgh: Banner of Truth Trust, 1982.

Murray, Iain Hamish, and London Trust. *Revival And Revivalism: The Making And Marring Of American Evangelicalism 1750-1858*. Edinburgh: Banner of Truth Trust, 1994.

Orr, J, Edwin. "Wales Revival - The Awakening of 1904 in Wales - by J Edwin Orr - brought by Peter-John Parisis - founder of The School of Prayer : J. Edwin Orr : Free Download & Streaming : Internet Archive." Internet Archive: Digital Library of Free Books, Movies, Music & Wayback Machine. http://archive.org/details/WalesRevival-TheAwakeningOf1904InWales-ByJEdwinOrr-BroughtBy_906 (accessed January 26, 2013).

Peckham, Colin N., and Mary Morrison Peckham. *Sounds From Heaven: The Revival On The Isle Of Lewis, Scotland, 1949-1952*. Fearn: Christian Focus, 2004.

Pratt, Josiah, and Jonathan Edwards. *The Life of The Rev. David Brainerd, Missionary To The North American Indians*. London: R.B. Seeley and W. Birnside, 1834.

Purves, Jock. *Studies On The Scottish Covenanters*. Modbury, S. Aust.: Gould Genealogy & History, 2010.

Richardson, Don. *Peace Child*. Glendale, Calif.: G/L Regal Books, 1974.

Richardson, Don. *Eternity In Their Hearts*. Rev. ed. Ventura, CA: Regal Books, 19841981.

Roberts, Richard Owen. *Repentance: The First Word Of The Gospel*. Wheaton, Ill.: Crossway Books, 2002.

Rosenberg, Joel C.. *Implosion: Can America Recover From Its Economic And Spiritual Challenges In Time?*. Carol Stream, Ill.: Tyndale House Publishers, 2012.

Rushdoony, Rousas John, and Gary North. *The Institutes Of Biblical Law*. United States: Presbyterian and Reformed Pub. Co., 1973.

Rushdoony, Rousas John, and Herbert W. Titus. *The Institutes Of Biblical Law*. Vallecito, Calif.: Ross House Books, 1999.

Rushdoony, Rousas John. *To Be As God: A Study Of Modern Thought Since The Marquis de Sade*. Vallecito, Calif.: Ross House Books, 2003.

Schaff, Philip. *Creeds of Christendom: With A History And Critical Notes*. 6th ed. Grand Rapids: Baker Book House, 1983.

Schama, Simon. *The Embarrassment of Riches: An Interpretation of Dutch Culture In The Golden Age*. New York: Vintage Books, 19971987.

"St. Charles Lwanga and CompanionsMartyrs of Uganda - Saints & Angels - Catholic Online." Catholic Online. http://www.catholic.org/saints/saint.php?saint_id=35 (accessed January 26, 2013).

Strobel, Lee. *The Case For Faith: A Journalist Investigates The Toughest Objections To Christianity*. Grand Rapids, Mich.: ZondervanPublishingHouse, 2000.

The Westminster Confession of Faith: The Larger And Shorter Catechisms, With The Scripture-Proofs At Large.. Edinburgh: Printed by Mark and Charles Kerr, 1793.

Chicago formatting by BibMe.org

ABOUT THE COVER

The Midway Congregational Church in Liberty County, Georgia, located half way between Savannah and Darien. The Midway community was founded by thirty-eight Calvinistic families in 1752, and was the site of much revival prayer and consequent revival. The church functioned from 1752 to around 1865 and never had more than one hundred members at any one time, and only one thousand members in her history. Yet the Midway Church sent one hundred of her men in pastoral and evangelistic ministry. These men included Abiel Holmes, father of author Oliver Wendall Holmes and grandfather of Supreme Court Justice Oliver Wendall Holmes; Jedediah Morse, the father of artist and inventor of the telegraph Samuel F. B. Morse; Louis Leconte whose children were great scientists and physicians; Charles C. Jones, the "apostle" to the slaves of Coastal Georgia; and Daniel Baker, the mighty evangelistic preacher. Lyman Hall and Button Gwinnett, two of the three signers of the Declaration of Independence also hailed from Midway.

ABOUT THE AUTHOR

Pastor Baker is ordained in the PCA and has been in the ministry for over 30 years. A graduate of the University of Alabama, he received his M.Div. degree from Reformed Theological Seminary in Jackson, MS. His ministry is in Birmingham, AL serving in many areas as an Evangelist with Presbyterian Evangelistic Fellowship (PEF) and as Director of the Alabama Church Planting Network (ACPN). Prior to this he was Senior Pastor at Christ Community in Harftord, CT; Senior Pastor of Golden Isles Presbyterian Church for 10 years; and while there, he served as Board Chairman of The Whitefield School from 1994-2002. Al has been actively involved in foreign missions to Central America, Africa, The British Isles, Asia and the Far East. Al and his wife, Wini, have been married over 37 years and have three grown children, Andrew, Allen and Jeff, and eight precious grandchildren.112